THE

10 Best Decisions a Graduate Can Make

BILL & PAM
FARREL

HARVEST HOUSE PUBLISHERS

EUGENE, OREGON

Cover design by Left Coast Design, Portland, Oregon

Cover photo © Natalia Natykach / Shutterstock

Published in association with the literary agency of Alive Communications, Inc., 7680 Goddard Street, Suite 200, Colorado Springs, CO 80920. www.alivecommunications.com.

THE 10 BEST DECISIONS A GRADUATE CAN MAKE
Copyright © 2012 by Bill and Pam Farrel
Published by Harvest House Publishers
Eugene, Oregon 97402
www.harvesthousepublishers.com

ISBN 978-0-7369-4393-2 (pbk.)
ISBN 978-0-7369-4394-9 (eBook)

To all those who were in our youth ministry when
we were youth pastors, all who were youth in
the church when Bill was the pastor, and all the
remarkable interns serving at Love-Wise:

Thanks for sharing your life with us.
We keep you in our hearts and prayers.

*It is right for me to feel this way about all of you,
since I have you in my heart.*

—PHILIPPIANS 1:7

~

And to Eden and Callan, our granddaughters:

You are preschoolers now but each and every day
we pray you will grow into young adults who make
great decisions and lead others to do the same.

Follow your parents' great example and wisdom,
and you will be on the path to success.

Love,
Nana and Papa

~

To our sons, Brock, Zach and Caleb, and to
our wonderful daughter-in-law, Hannah,

Thanks for being so transparent in sharing your lives
and your wisdom. It was a joy to include your words,
and in sharing your experiences, we hope many
graduates turn out as awesome as we think you all are.

We love you.

"This is a perfect gift with purpose for any grad. I know what I will be passing out for the graduates in our life...this book."—JIM BURNS, AUTHOR OF *THE PURITY CODE*

"In a world that says there's nothing for you after college but debt, recession, and unemployment, Pam and Bill Farrel challenge you to dream big! This book explains the dream and how to get there. A must read for any grad."—RENEE FISHER, SPEAKER AND AUTHOR OF *FAITHBOOK OF JESUS.*

"Bill and Pam Farrel are always filled with real-world advice that even I am able to put into practice. Help your graduate launch well—buy them this book!"—FRANK PASTORE, RETIRED PROFESSIONAL BASEBALL PITCHER AND RADIO TALK SHOW HOST

"A graduate needs vision, encouragement, and someone who believes in all that God has for them. Bill and Pam Farrel provide that and more in the pages of this book. It's a book every graduate deserves to read."—JILL SAVAGE, AUTHOR OF *MY HEART'S AT HOME*

"If you can buy only one gift for the grad on your list, then get a copy of this book. When the gift cards are empty and the pens are out of ink, this is one present that will last a lifetime."—ELLIE KAY, AMERICA'S FAMILY FINANCIAL EXPERT®

"Bill and Pam Farrel are so encouraging and wise in their advice that it keeps you coming back for more. Thanks for such needed practical advice, Bill and Pam."—CHAD EASTHAM, AUTHOR OF *THE TRUTH ABOUT GUYS*

Contents

@Tony Dungy
"It's about the journey—mine and yours—and the lives we can touch, the legacy we can leave, and the world we can change for the better."

@Muhammad Ali
"Impossible is just a big word thrown around by small men who find it easier to live in the world they've been given than to explore the power they have to change it. Impossible is not a fact. It's an opinion. Impossible is not a declaration. It's a dare. Impossible is potential. Impossible is temporary. Impossible is nothing."

@Deb and Jay Schroeder
"Make each day a masterpiece."

@Mahalia Jackson
"God can make you anything you want to be, but you have to put everything in God's hands."

Chapter 1

Decide to Go Big

Congratulations, graduate! This is a big moment in your life. One of many big moments to come. Our family knows something about big moments like graduations. The year we signed on to write this book, one son graduated from high school, another from college, and our oldest and his wife graduated with their master's degrees. We have been dreaming big dreams with them, and now we want to dream big with you.

You see, you were designed to think big and to live big. When you were very young, you invented worlds of fantasy and adventure and you regularly inserted yourself as the hero. God wants you to dream about what is possible with your life and to pursue goals that are big enough to motivate you.

KIDS DREAM BIG

Pablo Picasso said, "All children are artists. The problem is how to remain an artist once he grows up."[1] David Ewalt asked a second-grade class in New Jersey what they wanted to be when they grew up. The top three responses were superhero, firefighter, and policeman.[2] One youngster said he has wanted to be a cop since he was two so he could arrest his dad.[3]

None of these kids thought small. One of our sons told us at age two, "I want to be president of the world." Kids' minds are captivated with big possibilities and are good reminders of the innate drive we all have to think big.

Think back to when you were a young child. What did you want to be when you grew up? As you look forward to your life, deciding your major, what college or graduate school to attend, or what career path to take, never lose that sense of courageous adventure you had. You might not become "president of the world," but you can achieve many of those dreams—as long as you keep dreaming big.

Ask your friends and family if they remember what you said you wanted to be when you grew up.

To Go Big, Go for the Heart

"Get motivated."

"Get fired up."

"Focus."

"Get off your seat and do something."

We've all heard these words from coaches, parents, teachers, and others who care about us. They all point to the fact that life takes energy—a lot of energy.

God knows this, and when he wants to raise your energy level he puts a big desire on your heart.

When King Solomon was preparing to dedicate the newly built temple in Jerusalem, he recounted that the desire to build this temple had originated in the heart of his father: "My father David had it in his heart to build a temple for the Name of the LORD, the God of Israel" (1 Kings 8:17).

And generations later, when Nehemiah led the effort to rebuild the broken-down walls of Jerusalem in the face of intense opposition, he credited their success to the people's unwavering desire: "So we rebuilt the wall till all of it reached half its height, for the people worked with all their heart" (Nehemiah 4:6).

These were huge tasks with lots of obstacles that

needed "heart" to succeed. God is going to work in your life in the same way as long as your heart's desire is to please him.

"Take delight in the LORD, and he will give you the desires of your heart" (Psalm 37:4).

> "God deserves our very best, nothing more,
> nothing less, nothing else."—CHARLES SWINDOLL

It is vital that you pay attention to what God has put in your heart because he will use this passion to guide you into your future. It will also be the focal point of your greatest personal struggles because you live in a world that is trying to capture your heart. First John 2:15-17 admonishes us, "Do not love the world...For everything in the world—the lust of the flesh, the lust of the eyes, and the pride of life—comes not from the Father but from the world." Your world is trying to captivate you with experiences that ignite your senses, possessions that make you feel important, and short-term accomplishments that keep you focused on yourself. At the same time, God is trying to capture your heart with his purpose and desires that will build your life and future. You will have to choose every day which side you want to follow.

In this chapter, you are going to hear how God stirred the hearts of our three sons, Brock, Zachery and Caleb. It won't take you long to realize their passion is in sports but we don't want you to focus on the athletic part. Instead, look for the ways, the process, God used to inspire their hearts to live bigger lives. God will likewise put a desire on your heart that captures your interest and motivates you to invest time, energy and focus.

Going Big Sometimes Means Being a Leader—Brock

As I was growing up, my parents instilled in me the idea that I was a leader. They taught me that I was free in Christ to pursue excellence because I never had to worry that God would condemn me. They taught me that if I chose to embrace this pursuit, others would notice the quality of my life and want to follow my example.

I remember one high-school football game where the other team had just scored to take a five-point lead with sixty-one seconds left on the clock. Everyone on our team was discouraged thinking we were going to lose another game. I walked up and down the sidelines telling our players, "This is why we play this game. We are going to get the ball and drive down the field, score a touchdown, and win this contest." My teammates discovered renewed confidence. Leadership took us to a place we had not been before.

> "A leader's most powerful ally is his
> or her own example."—JOHN WOODEN

I'm now a football coach and it is just awesome to watch young men respond to leadership which helps them perform at a higher level. I had the opportunity to coach one of the best high-school quarterbacks in Virginia (who is now playing college ball). He learned sophisticated offensive schemes and inspired his team to play at a high enough level to win the state championship. At the beginning of the spring, these players had been a bunch of independent teenagers who had trouble focusing. By the end of the season, they were a unified team operating at championship caliber. The satisfaction in my heart was huge, and I realized I have the opportunity to develop this kind of character in young men for the rest of my life.

"When you dream you create a sky
where others are stars."—DENISE HOWARD

 If you make the choice to dream big, how might that help others also dream big?

Going Big Sometimes Means Changing Course—Caleb

As you make choices about your education and your career, you will most likely change your mind a number of times. You may try a field and find out it's not for you. Or you may take a risk only to watch everything fall apart in front of you. Don't get discouraged. Life is filled with possibilities, so setbacks don't have to define who you are.

> "Great necessities call forth
> great leaders."—ABIGAIL ADAMS

Sometimes the road ahead seems clear, but it turns out to be a detour that wakes you up to who you really are. During my senior year of high school, I was encouraged by my parents, teachers, and leaders at church to pursue an appointment to the Air Force Academy. My goal was to get a degree in engineering and play college football, and entering the academy seemed to everyone like my best shot to do both. Unfortunately, my SAT scores were a little too low, so I wasn't able to make it straight into the academy. I was offered a scholarship, however, to attend a military prep school. They had a decent football program and I was told, "If you keep your grades up, you will get in to the academy."

So off I went to the opposite coast with a sense of purpose and determination. I arrived early for the start of football camp, and I quickly felt I did not belong. I didn't expect to feel this way. It was an extremely stressful experience. It wasn't the school. The school was doing just what it promised, preparing leaders for careers in military leadership. And it wasn't that I was unprepared for being on my own. My parents travel most weekends, so I am more independent than my peers. I've held a job since I was sixteen, and I've served in numerous positions of leadership.

But I felt a heavy impression that I was not where God wanted me to be. It was one of the few times in my life when I felt like God was really talking to me. Every time I read my Bible, I got a strong sense that I didn't belong where I was. I believe that military service is a high calling, and the more I was surrounded by others who were clearly called, the more I was convinced I was not.

People would be disappointed if I left. I would have to engage in conversations with a string of respected authority figures whom I did not want to disappoint. But I wanted to please God more than any human person. I couldn't eat because of the stress, so I decided to fast for a few days. When I wasn't at football practice I was reading my Bible and praying. I felt desperate to know the mind of God. Because my father is a great counselor and a very godly man, I called him to pray and be a sounding board as I talked through the decision.

The more I prayed, the stronger that sense grew that this was not God's will for me. Then, on top of all that, I pulled my hamstring. With playing football now temporarily off the table, I checked myself out of school and flew home to regroup.

When I am in distress, I call to you,
because you answer me.—PSALM 86:7

I knew I had to get back on track quickly or this would end up being a bad chapter in my life with long-term consequences. I sought out the football coach at Grossmont Community College and told him my story. I finished rehab on my hamstring, but I was glad to be moving in the direction God wanted, even though I had to start the season late as the fourth string safety. The stress was gone and my energy was up, so I found plenty of determination to work as hard as necessary to make progress. By the end of the season, I had moved up to second string.

> Now to Him Who, by (in consequence of) the
> [action of His] power that is at work within us, is able
> to [carry out His purpose and] do superabundantly,
> far over *and* above all that we [dare] ask or think
> [infinitely beyond our highest prayers, desires,
> thoughts, hopes, or dreams].—EPHESIANS 3:20 AMP

I worked hard during the off-season and became a starter the next fall. A highlight from my final junior college game was returning an interception ninety-six yards for a touchdown in the playoffs. I sensed God's pleasure on me as I ran. I received a scholarship to play at Harding University in Arkansas where I'm now getting an excellent education in engineering. I do not yet know why God moved me from Track A to Track B, but I'm excited to see what the future has in store.

Who do you go to when you need a sounding board, someone to just listen and help you think through things? Ask your friends and family who they go to for advice and how they selected them.

Going Big Sometimes Means Believing the Impossible—Zachery

Going into my freshman year in high school, I was chubby, out of shape, and under motivated. As a result, even though I loved to play sports, I had a hard time adapting to high school football. But don't let anyone ever tell you that you can't do what your heart loves.

> "Keep away from people who try to belittle your ambitions. Small people always do that, but the really great make you feel that you too can become great."—MARK TWAIN

I started out as a third-string defensive lineman, but I had a hunch that I could be a lot better if I committed myself to improve my athletic performance. After freshman ball ended, I spent every waking hour I could in the weight room and dedicated myself to our school's agility program. I consulted with the varsity football coach on the best ways to get bigger, stronger, and faster. I discovered I had a pretty strong championship drive inside me. It needed to be cultivated and it needed to mature, but it was definitely there.

With renewed focus I set a big goal for myself: I wanted to make the varsity football team my sophomore year so I could compete with my older brother during his last year. No one thought it could happen, but they didn't realize how dedicated I was. Through many hardworking hours, I was able to transform my body into that of a varsity athlete. I was thrilled the next fall when the coach announced that I would be one of the starting outside linebackers.

What obstacles do you see on the road ahead? How can you fuel the fire inside you to achieve your dream? Talk with those you trust and ask them how they keep enthused to pursue the goals.

"Enthusiasm is the mother of effort, and without it nothing great was ever achieved."—RALPH WALDO EMERSON

As my confidence grew, I opened up to the possibility of being a competitive cheerleader. My mom had put me in gymnastics as a kid, and a number of football players were on the coed cheer team, so I figured I might be pretty good at it. Plus I was one of the few who could bench press over 350 pounds and also do a standing backflip. So I agreed to join the team.

I have struggled with ADD, and the intense schedule helped me focus by burning off the high energy that makes it hard for me to sit still and concentrate. So even though I was tired from all the practices, I actually did better academically.

Success Breeds Success

That year sparked my interest in what I am doing today. After my senior year, I accepted a cheerleading scholarship to the University of Louisville. I was asked to be the captain for four of the five years I competed, and we won the national championship all five of those years. While pursuing my degree, I discovered exercise science. The knowledge of how the body works in high-level athletic competition ignited something in me that made school easier and gave me the willingness to make the necessary commitments to succeed. I have now earned a master's degree and get to work full-time with college athletes as a performance coach.

As you get to know yourself, you are going to discover your passions. God stirs in you to perform at a high level in the areas of life that you love. "Whatever you do, work at it with all your heart, as working for the Lord" (Colossians 3:23). Give in to the motivation because God has good plans for you. If the dream excites you, step out and do it. Follow your heart.

> "Every great dream begins with
> a dreamer."—HARRIET TUBMAN

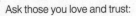

Ask those you love and trust:

- When I am excited about something, what does it look like?
- As you look back over the time you have known me, when have you seen me the most motivated?
- What things seem to suck the motivation out of me? (Remember, it is just as vital to know what to say no to.)

And God is able to bless you abundantly, so that in all things at all times, having all that you need, you will abound in every good work.—2 CORINTHIANS 9:8

You Live

"My parents gave me the freedom to follow my heart," Brock said in a Sunday morning message the week he graduated from high school. "I had a dream big enough to make good choices to achieve."

Brock kept the goal of playing and coaching football by having many items related to the sport in his room. Create something to remind you to dream big and follow your heart. Some ideas include:

- A screen saver
- A calendar
- A poster of you doing what you love

- A banner
- A T-shirt
- Something to set on your desk

Place that reminder where you can see it daily as you step out to follow your heart. Dream big!

 Go to www.Love-wise.com to find a photo with inspirational words you can use as a screen saver.

@Mary McLeod Bethune
"I always tell my graduating young people, 'Walk proudly in the light.'"

@Mary Kay Ash
"Don't limit yourself. Many people limit themselves to what they think they can do. You can do as far as your mind lets you. What you believe, remember, you can achieve."

@Jacqueline Kennedy Onassis
"We should all do something to right the wrongs that we see and not just complain about them."

Chapter 2

Decide to Use Social Media

O ur guess is you are actively involved with social media. You probably have accounts with Twitter, Facebook, YouTube, and Skype. You also likely own an iPhone, iPod, iPad, or something newer yet. Your world is so dominated by technology you might want to iconnect, ichat, icry, icare, and itouch to stay ihappy. And you hope your mistakes in the viral world do not lead you to say, "imsorry, iblewit, iwaswrong, or imstupid."

Technology and social media are the unique power apparatus of your generation. Consider the advantages you possess that no other generation before you could even imagine. You can:

- Follow a leader on Twitter and gain ongoing advice at no expense.

- Friend mentors, colleagues, acquaintances, or friends to keep track of their activities or gain insider information and wisdom.

- Reconnect with people without having to travel.

- Develop a professional web of potential opportunity.

- Skype with friends worldwide.

- Instantly share information and photos with the people who matter most to you.

The world is at your fingertips, and it is up to you to figure out how to use this potent gift. It will take thoughtful planning, discernment, and mature skills to harness its full potential.

> "With great power comes great responsibility."
> —SPIDERMAN'S WISE UNCLE BEN

The Good

My (Pam's) mentee, Renee Johnson Fisher, fostered relationships through Twitter, added in more influence using Facebook, and then extended her reach with a "Devotional Diva" blog written to encourage her peers. Her electronic footprint was used by God to connect Renee to a book agent. The result was the publication of her first book, *Faithbook of Jesus*, and an entire ministry to twentysomethings called Throw Mountains.[1] Living virally can cause movements of excellence and impact.

The Fever

Through the use of social media such as Twitter, Facebook and YouTube, Justin Bieber has become a pop star. When it was announced that he would be the headline act at Madison Square Garden, the show sold out in twenty-two minutes. His song, *Baby*, became the first video to earn half a billion views.[2] Twitter allows just 140 characters but has such impact.

> What are you posting? Write something that you think carries the message of your heart's desire (in a 140-character tweet):

Limitless Possibilities

Pull out that Smartphone. Social media is more powerful than any previous mode of mass communication because it has (notice what the bold-faced letters in the following acrostic spell):

- *Impact*: Any article, video, or audio you post can be linked by others and quickly go viral. Within a few days it can inspire the world.

- *Popularity*: As a leader, you can gather like-minded people who will follow your influence, team up on projects, and partner their friendship collection with yours for maximum impact.

- *Heart*: Skype sessions, emails, Facebook posts, and more keep people connected who would otherwise be out of touch. Those serving in the military or in missions can stay connected to those they love back home simply and instantly.

- *Organic*: Your social media accounts are reflections of you. You aren't creating a product, you are sharing you. As a result, any influence you have is a genuine extension of your personality, preferences, and principles. Since this is who you are, you will have no problem maintaining the influence.

- *Nano speed*: Your idea can move forward in a fraction of the time required by traditional communication and publishing. An idea can be planted into a tweet, posted on your status, included in a blog, and translated into an e-book. In a matter of weeks or even days, the literary genius in your head can be out changing lives while the traditional publishing timeline takes anywhere from months to years.

- *Eternal influence*: The influence of that summer mission trip can linger. You can continue to build relationships with the people you met while overseas, even though you are separated by several time zones.

> "How can you squander even one more day not taking advantage of the greatest shifts of our generation? How dare you settle for less when the world has made it so easy for you to be remarkable?"—SETH GODIN

Cyberskills for a Cyberworld

Anytime you work with something powerful, your skills need to be well trained. A race car driver needs much greater skills than the average freeway driver. In the same way, if you want to be effective with social media, you'll need to strengthen your abilities. To hone your skills, practice the "Beatitudes of Social Media" and process every post with discernment and wisdom:

The Beatitudes of Social Media

When using social media, you and those you are connected with will remain blessed or happy if you follow a few simple habits to harness the power:

- *Blessed are those who tweet unto others as you would have them tweet unto you.* It's just good common sense to use the Golden Rule (Luke 6:31) when posting anything about your family, friends, or acquaintances. Before you post, ask if this is something you would like said about you.

• *Blessed are those who use a GPS to post.* Ephesians 4:29 challenges us to only use words that are "helpful for building others up according to their needs, that it may benefit those who listen." Just like a GPS helps with directions, use your inner compass and before you post, ask if it shows respect for:

> **G**od
> **P**eople
> **S**elf

Erin Bury, Sprouter community manager, advises, "Don't say anything online that you wouldn't want plastered on a billboard with your face on it."[3]

• *Blessed are those who check with others before putting them in cyberspace.* Have a conversation with those you love about what posts, photos, and content they are comfortable having you share on your account or posting to theirs. Everyone's comfort level and privacy level is different.

• *Blessed are those who learn the tools of the trade.* It is wise to learn from those who already know. Find someone who knows the ins and outs of Twitter, Facebook, or whatever new social media has your interest and ask for guidance to get started. It's way easier to be coached ahead of time than to clean up a mess afterward.

- *Blessed are those who guard against hackers.* "If it looks like a hack, moves like a hack, it must be a hack." If a post looks different from what that friend usually posts, move with caution, especially if it looks like a movie, survey, or game application. Hackers are always coming up with new ways to gain access. If you happen to click on something harmful, quickly change your password, and then alert those who were affected.

- *Blessed are those who use direct message for private information.* The more important, volatile, or intimate the message, the more private the form of communication should be.

- *Blessed is the person who protects the pix.* Pictures posted should protect and honor the image of the people you friend at work, in the community, and at church. Facebook offers a "request to tag," which means you can send someone a picture privately for them to approve. If you don't like a photo of yourself that has been tagged, you can untag it, and it won't show on your page.

- *Blessed are those who work out issues offline.* Social

media is not the place to work out a personal problem. These technologies provide a casual environment for connecting with people at a simple level. Conflict resolution is a complex interaction that involves words, expressions, emotions, and sensitive expectations that are best handled face-to-face.

- *Blessed are those who bring good news.* Isaiah 52:7 reminds us, "How beautiful on the mountains are the feet of those who bring good news." Use the fruit of God's Spirit as a guide for social networking content, "love, joy, peace, forbearance, kindness, goodness, faithfulness, gentleness and self-control" (Galatians 5:22-23). Also, do not rob others from sharing their own good news. For example, let your friend announce her own engagement. If someone wins an award or gets a promotion, ask first before you take the joy he or she might get from telling others the exciting news.

- *Blessed are those who post helpful information.* Including links that may improve someone's quality of life or strengthen them spiritually can be used by God to dramatically help others.

- *Blessed are those who challenge others to think.* Proverbs 27:17 says, "As iron sharpens iron, so one person sharpens another." Social media is the new talk radio or public square of opinion. When you present views on public issues with reasonable logic and reliable facts, you help everyone be a little smarter.

- *Blessed are those who post using reasonable icons.* ☺ Icons are great for emphasis, and we all use them. But if you use them too frequently, people will grow bored and quit listening. AND IF YOU POST EVERYTHING IN ALL CAPS, PEOPLE WILL THINK YOU ARE YELLING.

- *Blessed are those who share tasteful humor.* The world can be a negative, harsh place so people appreciate well-placed levity. Proverbs 17:22 reminds us, "A cheerful heart is good medicine, but a crushed spirit dries up the bones."

Which social media beatitude do you want to apply to your life first?

Post with Discernment

No generation has been as vulnerable with personal information as your generation. Social media exposes anything you post to the entire world. That is why becoming socially *SHREWD* when it comes to online connections will be one of your greatest assets.

- *Safety first.* Don't reveal every place you are going or announce when you are on vacation. You lose control over who can be involved in your life and set yourself up to be taken advantage of.

- *Humor can hurt as well as heal.* Do not use humor at others' expense. Humor ceases to be funny when it demeans, hurts, or derides a person's character.

- *Reputations are made or broken through social media.* Everything you post will be checked out by people who want to know if they can trust you. Romantic interests, admissions offices, coaches, and employers will look at your social media sites. Out of work and out of love is a lonely place to be.

- *Emotions don't get expressed well through social media.* Even with uppercase sentences, italics, bold facing, or fancy fonts, the nuances of emotions don't come through clearly on electronic communications. Save your more precious emotional moments for when you are face-to-face.

- *Waiting is always better than rushing.* Think before you click "send." If in doubt, wait it out. Hold the message for twenty-four hours and pray it through. To err is human, but to hit delete is divine.

- *Damage can seldom be undone.* The power and speed of social media requires discernment in the way you send or post. From the moment a post or photo goes viral, it is live and it may never be recoverable no matter how quickly you hit the trashcan or delete button. If you do make a mistake, quickly delete, and let others know who might be affected.

Look at your social-media safety. Would any recent posts place you at risk socially, physically, or professionally?

THE ELECTRONIC GIANT

- Consumer research firm Nielsen found that the average Facebook user was on the site for a staggering six hours and thirty-five minutes per month, five times as much as they spent on Google.[4]

- University of New Hampshire researchers discovered, "Facebook and YouTube are the most popular social media platforms with college students. An astounding 96 percent of students said they use Facebook on a typical day and 84 percent use YouTube."[5]

- College students appear to be way beyond typical. Facebook user Courtney Bryson asked other college students to estimate their usage per week. The average estimate was between twenty to thirty hours a week on Facebook, not including other online activity.[6]

- One recent study tracked teens' usage of television and computer screens and discovered one-third are in front of the screen nearly forty hours a week.[7]

- As of March 2011, 175 million people had opened a Twitter account.[8]

- The average teenager watches about three-and-a-half hours of TV per day.[9]

- The average teen sends or receives 3,339 text messages per month.[10]

- The average teen invests fourteen hours per week playing video games.[11]

  In other words, your generation is using social media—a lot.

"Once you can understand where the conversation is, who leads, the type of voices and the best place for you to add your voice, you can then start becoming a more active participant."—MITCH JOEL

Is Social Media Robbing Your Relationships?

Social media is so powerful that it has the ability to become an obsession for some and an all-out addiction for others. Psychologist Sara Marcus points out that it becomes problematic when teens begin to ignore the real world: "They're not interacting with family as much. They're less interested in outside activities that they liked previously. Perhaps less socially engaged in person."[12]

> "The social network feeds into a narcissist's MO perfectly by allowing people to broadcast themselves 24/7 on their own terms."—**LARRY ROSEN**

For some, the ego feed is more than they are able to resist. "Facebook is fast becoming the online hangout of a new Me Generation—and that's not always a healthy thing," says Dr. Larry Rosen. A new study has found that teens and young adults who spend incessant amounts of time on the social-networking site are more prone to narcissism. "It is an excellent venue to promote me, me, me."[13]

Review your last few days of social media and see how many posts are about you and how many are aimed to help or applaud others?

Can You Unplug?

The growth of social media has also ushered in the growth of Facebook dysfunction:

- Relationships on Facebook have a seductive, addictive quality that can erode or even replace real-world relationships. An article published earlier this year in *European Psychiatry* presented the case of a woman who lost her job to a Facebook addiction. (She couldn't even make it through an examination without checking her Facebook account on her phone.)

- One-third of women in another study checked Facebook even before they went to the bathroom in the morning.[14]

- Aryn Karpinski, a researcher in the education department at Ohio State University, discovered that students who used Facebook had a "significantly" lower grade point average. "It is the equivalent of the difference between getting an A and a B."[15]

"Being true to ourselves doesn't make us people of integrity. Charles Manson was true to himself, and as a result, he rightly is spending the rest of his life in prison. Ultimately, being true to our Creator gives us the purest form of integrity."—JOHN WOODEN

Review the list below to see if you are *too* connected. You might be addicted if:

* You have a Facebook hangover. You're staying up late at night, and it affects you negatively the next morning.

* You ignore real people in the room (parents, siblings, roommates) to connect with your cyberfriends.

* You feel compelled to interrupt your normal life (homework, class, social activities) to check your friends' posts or update your status.

* Setting your cell phone to silent makes you break into a cold sweat.

* You dig up old loves without regard for his or her current relationships, putting your need for connection over their need for commitment.

* You are living vicariously through others' posts and tweets because you think your life is dull and meaningless.

* Time spent online (tweeting, posting, or reading posts) is interfering with your work, school work, or relationship success.

* You conceal your social media use or the amount of time spent playing online games.

* You get jealous of other people's plans and feel

left out even though you don't personally know them.

* You are putting your personal safety at risk to please an online connection by posting your every move and thought.

* You define your relationships by their Facebook status or judge your social status by your number of Facebook friends or Twitter followers.

TO FRIEND OR NOT TO FRIEND

1. Is this someone you have met in person and want to develop a more significant relationship with? *Friend*

2. Were you impressed when you met the person live? *Friend*

3. Is he or she a role model or mentor? *Friend*

4. Do you know his or her network of friends? *Friend*

5. Is he or she someone who shares your passions, politics, faith? *Maybe friend*

6. Does he or she have a love for your favorite hobby or activity? *Maybe friend*

7. Is this some random person and you have no idea how they found you? *Don't friend*

8. Are they saying inappropriate things to you or suggesting activities that make you uncomfortable? *Don't friend*

9. Are they asking for favors ("Bring me to your country" or "Send me money")? *Definitely don't friend*

10. Is he or she soliciting sex? *Run to the authorities!*

Log In or Log Out

You can take both preventative measures and corrective steps to keep your social media involvement healthy. Go to www.Love-Wise.com/gradplus and read what to do if you or a friend is over involved in social media.

It Is What You Make of It

We are social media users. We make use of Facebook, Twitter, LinkedIn, YouTube, and various RSS feeds. We regularly write blogs. We get it that social media is a great tool and that it's here to stay as we take this connected journey together. Technology, like dynamite, has power to remove obstacles or destroy opportunities. How will you use it?

You Live

Live it out in one of these areas:

- Review your balance of face time versus social media time. Do you need to make adjustments for a more balanced approach to building your network and living your life?

- How can you improve your online network or presence? Do you have posts or photos to remove? Do you need to gain a skill to best use an Internet tool (Facebook, Twitter, LinkedIn, Outlook/email, and Smartphone)?

- Look at your postings. Do they carry the message of your value system and core beliefs? Do you need to remove some of your posts or some of what your friends have posted?

- Is there a skill you want to gain to improve your people skills on- and off-line?

Share with a friend, mentor, or parent your goals as a result of reading this chapter. Ask for their input with this question, "Do you have any advice that you think would strengthen my social media network?"

Go to www.Love-Wise.com and read one article by Pam and Bill to improve your relationships *live*—face-to-face.

@Aristotle
"Educating the mind without educating the heart is no education at all."

@Eugene Swearingen
"The way to get to the top is to get off your bottom."

@Confucius
"Choose a job you love and you will never have to work a day in your life."

@Socrates
"Let him that would move the world first move himself."

Chapter 3

Decide to Follow Your Heart

Y ou have many important questions on your heart, such as:

- Whom will I marry?
- What career should I pursue?
- Where is the best place for me to live?
- What kind of ministry would be most effective for me to get involved with?
- Who are the friends I can trust?
- How should I spend my money?

Many of these questions are beyond your ability to figure out on your own. In order to choose wisely on all these issues every time, you would need a perspective that can see into the future. You don't have that kind of vision, but God does. Sometimes, God will move your heart in order to move you forward in your journey.

Get Your Heart in Motion

There are more than seven hundred references to the heart in the Bible. Proverbs 4:23 describes it as the well-spring of life from which vitality, wisdom, and morality are determined. It is a powerful force in our lives and, when illuminated by God's Spirit, it can see what our minds miss, which is why Paul prayed that "the eyes of your heart may be enlightened" (Ephesians 1:18).

> There are times when God needs to get us
> moving even though we don't understand
> all the reasons why. In those times God
> stirs our hearts as a call to action.

A Change of Heart

Today we have many ways to sway people's thinking: bumper stickers, T-shirts, Twitter, Facebook, billboards, press conferences, and talk show appearances. It's catchy and entertaining, but it's not always the truth. God is into giving real, substantial truth, not spin, to move our hearts—he gives *himself and his character* to back up every promise in the Bible. He moves the heart by showing us his love, power, and protection.

Like a computer's operating system running in the background while you're working, God's character is moving behind the scenes to support us and the plans he has for us. When God wants us to join him in one of his big adventures, he often does so by moving *our* heart with *his* character in *his* timing. When God rallied a group to go rebuild the temple, he did so with a heart movement: "everyone whose heart God had moved—prepared to go up and build the house of the LORD in Jerusalem" (Ezra 1:5).

(To read a devotional about more leaders who followed their hearts, go to www.Love-Wise.com/gradplus.)

A Boot Up for the Heart

God is preparing you now. At some point in your life, God is going to invite you into one of his big adventures. It will defy your imagination and probably involve some risk. On your own, you would never do it, so God will move your heart to get you to say yes. Once you have responded, your confidence will rise, your courage will ignite, and your commitment will never be in question.

There was a rule in the Pritchett household about computer games. You could play if you designed and built them yourself. The arrangement ignited something in Bob Pritchett: "When I was eight years old my dad brought home our first computer...This was the coolest thing—a machine you could program to do anything you wanted. All you had to do was tell it."

Bob became a whiz with his new technology. He

wrote his first program at age fifteen and at age seventeen he became the youngest programmer Bill Gates hired at Microsoft. Then God moved Bob's heart at age nineteen to write Logos Bible software, which quickly became a thriving corporation. The company is now the premier Bible software developer. Over 650,000 people worldwide subscribe to its service, and the company grew 40 percent in the year this book was written—in the middle of one of the worst global recessions of our time. The stirring of one young heart has now resulted in multitudes learning the good news of God's love. (Go to www.Love-Wise.com/gradplus to read how he did it.)

> Let no one look down on your youthfulness,
> but rather in speech, conduct, love, faith
> and purity, show yourself an example of
> those who believe.—1 TIMOTHY 4:12 NASB

Heart by Sunday

Sunday is twelve and the oldest of five children. He is raising his four siblings in Uganda because both his parents have died and are buried outside the door of their hut. It is hard to imagine where someone who hasn't even reached his teens finds the fortitude to tackle such overwhelming circumstances, but painted on the side of the hut is the simple phrase, "God is able."[1]

When the heart is prompted by God, an intense

desire to give rises up. "Everyone who was willing and whose heart moved them came and brought an offering to the Lord" (Exodus 35:21).

God will, at the right time and for the right reasons, move your heart to do something that is both bigger than you and honoring to him. As you step into the place God has called your heart to be, you too will be able to proclaim, "God is able."

With friends and family, ask these questions:

- Have you ever felt moved to do something and at first you didn't know why?

- Do you have a story to tell me about a time when God "was able" in your life?

- Share with them a time in your life when you felt God stir your heart.

- Make a list of ten causes, charities, or nonprofits you believe in. Share your list and see what organizations they donate to and why.

Face Down Fear of the Future

It's normal to be a mix of emotions right now. You might feel excitement over the wonderful achievement of graduation—and you should. According to the U.S. Census Bureau, 84 percent have high school diplomas while only 27 percent have college diplomas.[2] Even fewer go on to achieve a master's, PhD, or equivalent.

Excited? Yes! However, it is also normal to have a few apprehensions because of the unknown ahead.

> "You gain strength, courage, and confidence
> by every experience in which you stop and
> look fear in the face…you must do the thing you
> think you cannot do."—ELEANOR ROOSEVELT

We know what it is like to feel fear as you graduate. My (Pam) senior year was very unpredictable. My father was a brilliant businessman, but he struggled with alcoholism. When he drank, he became more and more depressed and often suicidal. The future seemed unsure to me. My parent's marriage was hanging by a thread. Soon after, despite my father's drinking, he was promoted at work and my family moved away. I had to make many more choices. Would I stay in the city I grew up in and go to college? Would I go with my family to a new city for college? Would I go away to even another city for school? Would my parents make it? Would there be funds for college if a divorce happened? Given his downward spiral, would my dad be alive to see me graduate from college? And (oh, yeah) what am I supposed to major in?

I (Bill) was equally unsure at graduation. My mother struggled with emotional stability which made my life unpredictable. She moved me right before my senior year. Then two months from graduation, my father suffered a stroke that left him paralyzed. While I somehow managed to get a near perfect score on my math SAT exam, I elected to stay close to home and attend a junior college to help my father rehabilitate. I had no idea how God was going to get me to the finish line of a college degree when so much was unstable at home.

But God was faithful. Even with the foundations of each of our lives shaking under us, we found hope and direction. For me (Pam), God sent a friend (appropriately named Grace), who invited me to a Campus Crusade for Christ meeting. There I met a godly mentor and learned how to study the Bible to discern God's will. I saw that if I had an accurate (BIG) view of God, my heavenly father would step in and lead me.

I (Bill) was introduced to that same ministry where I discovered new tools for digging into God's Word. I gained courage and direction day after day. From two separate college campuses, God sent us to the same leadership conference where we separately decided God was calling us into ministry—then God introduced us to each other. While we didn't know everything, we knew enough to get started.

For the LORD will be your confidence.
—PROVERBS 3:26 NASB

What are you most excited about in your future? What are you most afraid of about your future?

To face down fear, write down as many traits and names of God as you can think of. To help, you might want to go A to Z (God is **a**mazing, **b**eautiful, **c**aring, **d**ivine, and so on). Select one trait and hang your heart on it. Look up verses with that word in it. To help you find verses, go to Biblegateway.com or ask for Logos Bible Software for a graduation gift.[3] Now personalize the verses. Place your name right in it, print it out on your computer and frame it. Post it someplace you can see it. Read the truth out loud and watch your courage soar.

Go to www.Love-wise.com/gradplus for a Scripture prayer ready for you to use today.

Over dinner, also ask your friends and family to share times when they saw God show up big on their behalf, or how he led them in times they were confused or afraid.

"Be strong and courageous. Do not be afraid or terrified...for the LORD your God goes with you; he will never leave you nor forsake you."—**DEUTERONOMY 31:6**

Respect the Power of the Heart

Your heart is like a sports car with a powerful engine. I (Bill) had the opportunity once to drive a Porsche 911. When sports cars stay on the road, it's a thrill to be in the seat feeling the rush of power. When the car goes out of control at full throttle, however, it's a disaster. Protect your heart with these quick questions:

1. Did I think it through?

Headlines scream it every day: Three young adult siblings rob a bank and shoot at a police officer as they seek to escape. Twentysomething Casey Anthony parties when her three-year-old daughter is missing. Lindsay Lohan, whose bank account is piled high, swipes a $2500 necklace while shopping. These examples make us all ask, "What were they thinking?"

If you ever come up with a plan that is radically different from what most people think is wise, you might want to run that plan by friends, family, mentors, and role models first. "The heart is deceitful above all things and beyond cure. Who can understand it?" (Jeremiah 17:9).

2. Did I test it?

Anything worthwhile in life gets tested. Throughout your education, you have taken tests to see if the knowledge you were gaining actually stuck. Without tests, you would not know for sure if you had truly learned what you set out to discover.

Imperfect King David was declared a man after God's own heart in large part because he welcomed this testing process in his life: "I know, my God, that you test the heart and are pleased with integrity" (1 Chronicles 29:17). When God commissioned the prophet Jeremiah, he said to him, "I the LORD search the heart and examine the mind, to reward each person according to their conduct, according to what their deeds deserve" (Jeremiah 17:10).

Inviting God to regularly examine your heart is one of the smartest decisions you will ever make, "for the LORD searches every heart and understands every desire and every thought" (1 Chronicles 28:9). It isn't as though you are hiding anything from him, because he already knows. Your willingness to be tested opens you up to the intimacy and blessing of having a close relationship with God.

God wants to test your heart because he wants the best for you.

3. Am I paying attention?

Signing up for your test is not difficult. You just need to pay attention to God's Word. "For the word of God is alive and active. Sharper than any double-edged sword, it penetrates even to dividing soul and spirit, joints and marrow; it judges the thoughts and attitudes of the heart" (Hebrews 4:12).

Some of the passages you read will make you feel better about yourself as God uses them to encourage you and give you strength for the next challenge of your life. You will want to record these somehow. Write them on the desktop of your computer or phone. Post them on your mirror to remind you that God has your back.

Other verses are going to bother you. They may seem confusing or irritating or you may feel they have probed your soul. These verses are pointing to the next area of growth. As you pay attention, you gain wisdom on how God wants to help you be your best. You will want to catalog these passages also. Though they may not be as clear as the verses that make you feel good, they are calling you to change and are just as important.

4. Is my heart divided?

Am I saying one thing and doing another? Like these examples from the news:

* A twenty-six-year-old animal research technician pleaded guilty to taking the life of a graduate student.

* A board member for a healthcare organization has a restraining order issued against her for allegedly assaulting several security guards.

* A policeman was charged with cheating at a casino and drunken driving.

* A man with a Bible verse tattooed on his forehead was charged with assault and battery.

Pray this:

> Teach me your way, LORD,
>   that I may rely on your faithfulness;
> give me an undivided heart,
>   that I may fear your name.
>   (Psalm 86:11)

And the results are good:

> They will have no fear of bad news;
>   their hearts are steadfast,
>   trusting in the LORD.
>   (Psalm 112:7)

Choose what kind of a heart you want to have.

You Live

Lou Holtz, the only football coach in NCAA history to lead six different programs to bowl games, defines the word *win* as a question: "**W**hat's **I**mportant **N**ow?"

Choose one decision in this chapter to keep your heart soft toward God and his best plan for your life.

 Go to www.Love-Wise/gradplus to read stories of others who have followed when God stirred their heart.

@Dennis Fisher
"Each of us has been given gifts; and when we use them for God's glory, they bring satisfaction and joy."

@Aristotle
"We are what we repeatedly do. Excellence, then, is not an act, but a habit."

@Booker T. Washington
"Success is to be measured not so much by the position that one has reached in life as by the obstacles which he has overcome trying to succeed."

@Moses (Psalm 90:12)
"Teach us to number our days, that we may gain a heart of wisdom."

Chapter 4

Decide to Be Skilled

In case you haven't heard it recently, you are entering a world that can be tough, discouraging, and frustrating. For example, 80 percent of college grads moved back home in 2009 until they landed a full-time job.[1] Only 44 percent of employers say they will hire a new college graduate, and with five applicants for every one job,[2] it can take months—or longer—to get the job you dream of. In addition, most college grads today have $20,000 plus in educational debt.[3] A *Time* magazine article underscores the financial challenges you face today, "Only half of Americans in their twenties earn enough to support a family, or consider themselves financially independent."[4]

Not only are recent graduates competing against each other for fewer jobs, but they're also up against more-experienced workers who graduated a few years before them and are back in the job market.[5]

Choose to be the best and gain the edge with excellence.

> "The roots of true achievement lie in the will to become the best you can be."—HAROLD TAYLOR

Compete to Win

You have no choice but to be a highly skilled competitor. You are working hard to build a successful life while there are forces at work creating obstacles all along the way.

> "Keep your face to the sunshine and you cannot see the shadows."—HELEN KELLER

Get the Right Kind of Calluses

We know a young lady who was the runner-up for the U.S. Olympic gymnastics team. Her callused hands equipped her to compete at the highest level. A callused heart, however, would have stopped her. Consider the ways that a hardened heart ruined people's lives in the Bible. It makes people:

- *Irritating*: Pharaoh became an obstinate enemy of God by stubbornly refusing to let the people of Israel leave and suffered the loss of his oldest son as a result. He was so stubborn that "the LORD hardened Pharaoh's heart" (Exodus 11:10). We are all told in 1 Samuel 6:6 that we are capable of hardening our hearts in the same way.

- *Irrational*: Psalm 95:8 states, "Do not harden your hearts as you did at Meribah." The story is told in Exodus 17:1-7. The Israelites had seen the miraculous plagues that secured their deliverance from Egypt and manna from heaven to feed them daily. After all that, they panicked because there was no water in sight. Rather than seek God for an answer, they grumbled to Moses, "Why did you bring us up out of Egypt to make us and our children and livestock die of thirst?" (v. 3). Really? It appears when your heart calluses over, your mind loses its ability to think clearly.

- *Incapacitated*: Hebrews 3:7-8 says, "Today, if you hear his voice, do not harden your hearts." "Follow me, come this way, stay away from that, let me help you," are common phrases for the Holy Spirit. He always gives advice to help us be our best. When our hearts are soft, we hear and willingly follow. When our hearts are hardened, we lose our hearing.

- *Inferior*: Jeremiah 5:23 reports the activity of a callused heart, "But these people have stubborn and rebellious hearts; they have turned aside and gone away." Rather than stick with the smartest, strongest, wisest, most insightful Person ever, they chose to follow the small and deceptive schemes of men.

You have worked hard to get where you are, and we doubt any of you have it as your goal to be stubborn, irrational, spiritually deaf, or on an inferior team. It is simply what happens when you give up on your goals and allow your heart to harden.

Stepping Up to Your Goals

Goals don't have to be intimidating. Goals are simply a set of steps. One after another, these steps will get you from where you are now to where you want to be.

Choose a goal. The process begins by choosing something you want to accomplish. Don't worry about whether you will get it perfect, just choose something. It is still true that you can't steer a parked car, so the main reason for choosing a goal is to keep you moving so God can guide your steps.

Create your worksheet. Draw a stair-step pattern on a sheet of paper. At the top of the stairs, write down in the simplest terms possible the goal you want to accomplish.

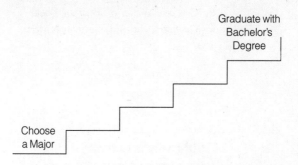

Catalog the steps. Brainstorm the steps you will need to take to accomplish your objective. For instance, if you want to graduate with a bachelor's degree you will need to:

- Choose a major
- Meet with a counselor
- Register each semester
- Pursue financial aid
- Ask other students for advice
- Evaluate your major periodically
- Schedule your time so you get your school work done

Coordinate your commitments. Once you have a list of the steps that will get you to your goal, put them in order and commit to the process of growth.

Try it. Do the stair step for *one* of your goals then have someone you trust check your work.

> "Joy comes from using your potential."—WILL SCHULTZ

STUPID THINGS THAT WILL MAKE A MESS OF YOUR LIFE
(observed by Farrels and friends):

- Eat only Wheaties and Mountain Dew. This is not a healthy diet. A friend's appendix burst after eating this way for two straight years on campus.

- Do dishes only once a month so mold grows on them.

- Get angry often. Others will think you're a real jerk and avoid you at all costs.

- Read Facebook for your daily devotions.

- Use your roommate's toothbrush or shower loofa.

- Wear your roommate's clothes and jewelry without asking so many times that when the real owner borrows them back, you get mad at her for borrowing "your stuff."

- Let your boyfriend/girlfriend sleep over and "accidently" walk in when roomies are in the shower.

- Take a car, bike, laptop, or anything without asking. It's even worse if you break it.
- Take money from your roomies and never repay them.

Any of these things will make others on campus *run* away from you.

> "Know who you are and what
> you believe."—GENA ROGERS

Active Decision-Making

Instead of allowing the bumps and bruises of life to callus your heart, move your life forward with some powerful decision-making.

Decision-Making Skill 1: The Obvious Test

Before you put a lot of effort into any decision, ask yourself, "Is this decision so obvious that I'm wasting time thinking about it?"

Decision-Making Skill 2: The Wisdom Test

Most decisions are not that obvious so you have to engage in some level of discovery, deliberation, and discernment. The Wisdom Test, therefore, consists of questions. If you answer yes to all these questions, it's pretty clear you ought to proceed. If you answer no to all of them, it is pretty clear you ought to back off.

If the obvious test doesn't make your decision clear, ask the following questions:

- Does this decision line up with my convictions?

- Will the people I respect most agree with this decision? Have I asked them?

- Is this decision based on healthy boundaries that will produce self-respect?

- Will this decision cause personal growth in my life?

- Would I encourage my best friends to make this same decision?

- Will this improve my most important relationships?

Decision-Making Skill 3: The Priority Test

If you've gone through The Obvious Test and The Wisdom Test, but you still need more evidence that you are making the best decision, use The Priority Test.

Step 1: Write out your decision in a positive way. Describe the decision before you in terms of what you will do if you say yes to it. For instance, "I'm thinking about renting an apartment and looking for a couple of roommates." This is better than, "I need to get out of my parents home because they are driving me crazy."

Step 2: Make a pro/con list. Create two columns on

a sheet of paper. On one side, write down the reasons why you *ought* to take this course of action. On the other side, write down the reasons why this course of action is *not* a good idea.

Step 3: Prioritize the reasons. In both columns, prioritize the reasons you have listed with an A, B, or C. Assign an A to the vital reasons you identify on your list. The supportive reasons get a B. And give a C to the reasons you came up with because you're creative and can come up with ideas that don't really affect the decision.

Step 4: Compare the high-priority reasons from both lists. Evaluate the A reasons for saying yes with the A reasons for choosing no. If it's a tie, then move to the B reasons to see if the decision becomes clearer. Don't be fooled by quantity. It's quite possible that one list will have more reasons than the other, *but quantity is no substitute for quality*, and decisions such as this require high-quality conclusions.[6]

Gather those you most trust to be a good sounding board for your decisions. Lay out your top three choices for one of these decisions and get their feedback:

- How to spend your summer

- What to major in

- Where to apply for work

- What to do after graduation: College, military service, trade or vocational school, travel?

"The remarkable truth is that our choices matter; not just to us and our own destiny but amazingly, to God Himself and the universe He rules."—PHILIP YANCEY

Kicking It in Kentucky—Zachery

In most of our decisions, we don't get to look down the road to see how it will turn out. We just have to gather whatever evidence we can, ask the people we respect, and then commit to something. As I was approaching my high school graduation, I had two options to go to school on an athletic scholarship. The first was an opportunity to play football at a smaller school. The reasons I had for saying yes were:

- I knew the head coach and had a lot of respect for him.

- It was relatively close to my home.

- I had a couple of friends who went to school there.

- It was a Christian school so I knew the morals and teaching would be strong.

The second was an opportunity to be on the coed cheer squad at the University of Louisville. The reasons I had for saying yes were:

- I had a relationship with the head coach because he had led training camps for our high school team.

- Louisville was one of the top cheerleading programs in the country.

- I knew I could get a high-quality education.

- I had a few friends who were already cheerleaders there.

- Living costs were cheaper in Kentucky.

Neither of these was obviously better than the other. The smaller school was attractive because it was Christian based, but Louisville was attractive because it was so competitive. I prayed and asked others, but in the end it was my decision to make. It was the first time in my life I remember thinking, *This is on me. I don't really know what's best for me, but I have to choose and then live with the decision.*

After a lot of question asking and prayer, I decided to go to the University of Louisville, primarily because of the strong reputation of the cheer program and the exercise science major I wanted. These were the strongest A reasons to me. However, I had to find ways to stay close to God in a secular environment, so I used the wisdom test to find ways to do that too.

When you are faced with the next big decision in your life, ask the people you respect the most, commit it to prayer, but then take a risk. Just the fact that you made a decision will raise your confidence, sharpen your focus, and increase your commitment level, which are three of the most important ingredients of success.

College Clarity Chart

Our advice is to create a chart or grid, such as the following, to help you evaluate the college, trade school, military academy, apprenticeship, professional certification program or graduate school you're interested in. (Go to www.Love-Wise.com/gradplus to see example.)

Give each characteristic a priority score of A, B, or C. Then assign a number value for each characteristic for each school—a 3 for an A priority, a 2 if it's a B, and a 1 if it's a C. Then add up the totals and set your sights on the schools that have the highest scores.

Following our oldest son's high school graduation, one of his friends went into the military, another became an electrical apprentice, one entered the police academy, and our son chose the traditional higher education route. You can also start your own business. There are many routes to success.

> "Do all the good you can by all the means you can in all the ways you can in all the places you can to all the people you can as long as you can."—JOHN WESLEY

My College Decision	Priority (A, B or C)	Schools (write in your top choices)					
City size							
Geography							
Extracurricular							
Financial aid offer							
Relationships							
Proximity to home							
Rating							
Christian presence on campus							
Housing options							
Total:							

Characteristics (assign priority; Give 3 for A, 2 for B, 1 for C if the school meets this

How to Get Through College Faster and Save Money

Our daughter-in-law was an academic advisor for a respected Christian university, and she finished a four-year degree in just three years. We interviewed Hannah and include here some of her advice to save you time (and you and your parents money):

- *Set goals.* Getting through school begins with the intention to finish. Choose a date and a course of study to pursue. You can always change these as you go, but you need something to aim at if you are going to make progress quickly. "For this God is our God for ever and ever; he will be our guide even to the end" (Psalm 48:14).

- *Meet with an advisor* as often as necessary to stay on track.

- *Discuss your options with faculty members*. They have been at this for a long time and have helped lots of other students.

- *Plan out your program* (i.e., English 101 in the fall, English 102 in spring, and so on). Decide where and when you're taking each course.

- *Ask about prerequisites* to make sure that you take your courses in order. You don't want to get to your senior year and realize you were supposed to take Math 200 before your Business 300 course.

- *Take courses at a community college*. If you are attending a four-year college, you can do this during the summer and winter breaks or online. If you go to college out of state, enroll in courses in your home state so you pay in-state tuition.

- *If you pay for eighteen hours of credits, then take eighteen hours of credits*. It may be hard at the time, but you're paying for them, so you as might as well take them.

- *Work while you're in school* so you have money

for food and housing. Don't use student loans to pay for anything other than school and books. You'll regret it later. "The rich rule over the poor, and the borrower is slave to the lender" (Proverbs 22:7).

- *Check the library* to see if they have a copy of your textbook. You may be able to borrow it from the library and not have to buy one.

- *Decide to get your degree when you're young.* It's a lot of work to take classes year-round, but it's easier now than it will ever be.

For more ways to save even more money while in college go to www.Love-Wise.com/gradplus.

Scholarship Sweepstakes

College is pricey, but there is money out there if you're willing to work hard to research and apply for it. One of our friends, Kathy Hart, now teaches a *Scholarships Made Simple* seminar because she and her daughter, Natalie, worked diligently to garner $61,750 to launch her college career. Natalie was not a valedictorian, and did not secure an athletic scholarship. So if you think only the top student or the all-star athlete have a chance—think again. You might need to apply full-time effort to the advice they give, but if you treat getting scholarships as you would a career and put in the hours, it can pay off.

Whatever you do, work at it with all your heart, as working for the Lord, not for human masters, since you know that you will receive an inheritance from the Lord as a reward. It is the Lord Christ you are serving.—COLOSSIANS 3:23-24

Heart Produces Wisdom

The beginning of wisdom is this: Get wisdom.
Though it cost all you have, get understanding.
(Proverbs 4:7)

More than any generation who has ever lived, you need wisdom. You get exposed to more knowledge in a day than most people before you encountered in a year. Breakthroughs are creating moral dilemmas that were unthinkable before you were born. No other generation has had to ask such questions as, "Should we clone human beings?" "Should we choose the gender of our baby?" No other generation has had to ask, "With all the ways I can communicate with others, what's the most appropriate way to have this particular conversation?"

Then there's the security issue. The primary concern for previous generations was deciding whether they needed to lock their house. You have to protect your house, email, social media, bank accounts, and any other source of information that might be a part of your identity.

In such a world, wisdom is king. Wisdom is a gift God gives to those who ask: "If any of you lacks wisdom, you should ask God, who gives generously to all without finding fault, and it will be given to you" (James 1:5). Wisdom is different from knowledge. Knowledge is information stored in the brain; wisdom is the ability to apply that knowledge to specific situations in a skillful and beneficial way. Knowledge energizes our thinking; wisdom energizes our decisions.

Knowledge asks, "What?" Wisdom asks, "How?"

When Solomon was given the opportunity to lead the nation of Israel, God asked him what he wanted. Solomon's appeal was, "So give your servant a discerning heart to govern your people and to distinguish between right and wrong" (1 Kings 3:9). The wisdom that God granted to Solomon as a result of his request was highly valued and sought after by the rulers of other nations: "All the kings of the earth sought audience with Solomon to hear the wisdom God had put in his heart" (2 Chronicles 9:23).

Wisdom is the skill that makes everything else in your life work better and leads your decisions to create a bright future.

"The future belongs to those who believe in the beauty of their dreams."—**ELEANOR ROOSEVELT**

You Live

The way of fools seems right to them, but the

wise listen to advice.—**PROVERBS 12:15**

Throw a dinner party and invite those just ahead of you on the journey. Make a list of questions you'd like answers for—and ask the group to pray for you before the party's over.

 Go to www.Love-Wise.com/gradplus for more decision-making and goal-setting advice.

@Eleanor Roosevelt
"It is not fair to ask of others what you are unwilling to do yourself."

@C.S. Lewis
"Every time you make a choice you are turning the central part of you, the part that chooses, into something a little different than what it was before."

@Ellyn Sanna
"Even the smallest actions can affect the lives of many; like pebbles tossed in a lake, you never know where the ripples will end. So don't be afraid to try. Dare to make a difference."

Chapter 5

Decide to Be Real

People are counting on you. There is a group of people who love the way you talk, the way you lead, and the way you make them feel when they are around you. If they find out over time that you are who you appear to be, they will talk about you in very positive ways and seek to follow your example. If, on the other hand, they discover you are a manipulator, a self-centered fake, or a poser, they will become angry and disillusioned.

As a result, one of the most important questions you can ask is, "Who am I, really?" You are a three-dimensional person with a body, a soul, and a spirit. Your body is the vehicle that interacts with the world around you through your five senses. Your soul is the unique collection of thoughts, feelings, attitudes, and personality that make you who you are. As a rule, your soul tells your body what to do, but your soul is constantly fighting with itself.

Genia Obal shares the following story that illustrates this battle within all of us:

> Our seven-year-old daughter had just won two dollars for her memory work in Sunday school. After the morning service, the pastor's wife congratulated her.
>
> Our daughter proudly announced, "And I put it all in the morning's offering."
>
> "My, how wonderful!" the pastor's wife exclaimed. "I'm sure God will be pleased."
>
> "Yes," the child replied. "Now maybe God will let me do some of the things I want to do!"

> "Many persons have a wrong idea of what constitutes true happiness. It is not attained through self-gratification but through fidelity to a worthy purpose."—HELEN KELLER

The Soul Is Trainable—Sort of

Your soul is an amazing creation that gives you a unique voice, unique ways of thinking, a uniquely creative approach to life, and a sphere of influence that only you can have. The challenge is that your soul needs to be trained and your soul needs help.

For years, I (Bill) coached youth basketball teams my boys played on.

One year I drafted a young man named Seth. He was not a good athlete and was easily distracted. I would explain what I wanted him to do and he would stare up to the sky and say, "Okay coach." As soon as he went on the court, I could tell he had no idea what he was doing.

Fortunately, the soul is trainable—kind of. I created a defense that I affectionately called "The Fly Defense." I said to the team, "Guys, we're going to install a new defense today, and Seth here is the key to the whole thing. Seth, your job is to buzz around the court and try to land on the basketball. And it might be good if you actually buzz whenever you get close to members of the other team. You got it?"

"Okay coach."

Amazingly, it worked. During the next game, he ran around like a madman buzzing so loud I could hear him from the sidelines. The other team was so confused by his behavior that we outscored our opponent every quarter he was on the floor.

We were able to train Seth's soul to help him mesh with our team and we had a lot of fun with it, but we had no illusions of turning him into a competitive basketball player. To do that, we would've had to put something in him that could transform him with somebody else's ability. On his own it was impossible.

> "We have too many high-sounding words,
> and too few actions that correspond
> with them."—**ABIGAIL ADAMS**

The same is true of us. We can train our minds, emotions, and will to do what we know is right, but we are limited in what we can achieve. We can contain the battle for a while, but we can never defeat our imperfections. We need a transformation to truly live. We need the ability of Christ.

Fortunately when we yield to him, the Holy Spirit is placed in our hearts in seed form. You now have the choice to feed and cultivate spiritual power in your life. As the influence of the Spirit grows, it gains the ability to tell the soul what to do, which then tells the body what to do. As Paul says in Galatians, "So I say, walk by the Spirit, and you will not gratify the desires of the flesh. For the flesh desires what is contrary to the Spirit and the Spirit what is contrary to the flesh. They are in conflict with each other, so that you are not to do whatever you want" (Galatians 5:16-17).

When the Spirit is leading the charge, we actively live out what we say we believe because the power of Christ is making it happen.

Body, Soul, and Spirit (1 Thessalonians 5:19-24)

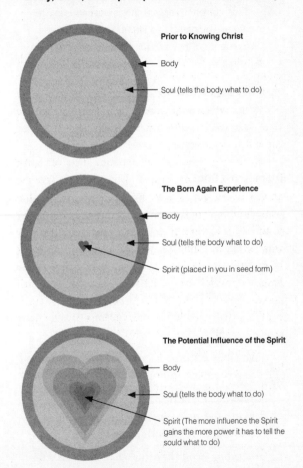

Prior to Knowing Christ

Body

Soul (tells the body what to do)

The Born Again Experience

Body

Soul (tells the body what to do)

Spirit (placed in you in seed form)

The Potential Influence of the Spirit

Body

Soul (tells the body what to do)

Spirit (The more influence the Spirit gains the more power it has to tell the sould what to do)

Is there a bad habit you can't seem to break? Or a good choice you can't seem to make a regular part of your life? Ask a mentor or older family member if they ever felt this way and what they did about it.

> "Someone once wrote, 'Sow a thought, reap an act. Sow an act, reap a habit. Sow a habit, reap your character. Sow your character, reap your destiny.'"—CHARLES SWINDOLL

Training the Soul

We are impressed with the rigorous training our brave servicemen and women go through to prepare to win their battles. In much the same way, you will want to diligently train your soul to live a victorious life.

> "Some people live an entire lifetime and wonder if they have ever made a difference in the world, but the Marines don't have that problem."—RONALD REAGAN

Take a look at the boot-camp like preparation God offers so you can live triumphantly:

- *Self-discipline.* Practicing a behavior twenty-one days in a row trains our soul to take ownership of it as a habit (1 Corinthians 9:24-27).

- *Goal setting.* We all have the ability to focus our

efforts by choosing deliberate pursuits (Philippians 3:12-14). (See the previous chapter on skills for developing a goal-setting plan.)

- *Wrestling with your thoughts.* Some thoughts will build us up while others tear us down. Personal growth involves a wrestling match that pins unhealthy thinking to the mat so it can't run our lives (2 Corinthians 10:5).

- *Creative problem-solving.* We all face situations that are either new to us or have nagged us for far too long. Since we have been made in the image of God and God is a creative being, we have the ability to synthesize information into new solutions (Genesis 1:27).

- *Accountability relationships.* Choosing people we must answer to for our actions can help produce healthy behavior. A boss at work, mentors in our personal development, and friends who ask us hard questions can all help us be better at what we do (Proverbs 27:17).

- *Formal training.* Educational programs, seminars, internships, and extracurricular commitments can hone our skills, expand our knowledge, and increase our effectiveness.

Making the Spirit Stronger in You

The Spirit is like a seed that gets put in the ground.

Its influence starts out small, but under the right conditions it will grow to be the best part of your life. You can create those conditions by PLANTing and WATERing.

First, PLANT God's Word into your life consistently:

Probe (2 Timothy 2:15, "a worker...who correctly handles the word of truth.") This is the process of studying God's Word so it makes sense to us.

Listen (Romans 10:17, "faith comes from hearing the message, and the message is heard through the word of Christ.") Hearing other people teach the Bible and relate how it is affecting their lives encourages growth in all of us.

Acquaint yourself (Deuteronomy 17:19, "he is to read it all the days of his life.") There is no substitute for reading God's Word consistently.

Nail it down (Psalm 119:11, "I have hidden your word in my heart.") Memorizing specific verses makes them readily accessible when we need them the most.

Think it over (Psalm 1:2, "Blessed is the one... who meditates on [God's] law day and night.") Asking questions like, "How do I live this out? And how does this apply to my life?" energize God's Word in our lives

Second, WATER your relationship with God through interactive prayer:

Wait for God (Romans 8:16, "The Spirit himself testifies with our spirit that we are God's children.") Listen in prayer by saying, "God, you go first," and then assume the thoughts that come to mind are what God wants to talk to you about.

Acknowledge your sin to God (1 John 1:9, "If we confess our sins, he is faithful and just and will forgive us our sins and purify us from all unrighteousness.")

Thank God (1 Thessalonians 5:18, "give thanks in all circumstances; for this is God's will for you in Christ Jesus.")

Exalt God (Psalm 103:1, "Praise the LORD, my soul; all my inmost being, praise his holy name.")

Request of God (Philippians 4:6, "in every situation, by prayer and petition, with thanksgiving, present your requests to God.")

Keep Breathing

When I (Pam) was a freshman in college, it seemed I followed a pattern of making one good choice and three dumb ones. I just couldn't move my life forward as I wanted. I went to church, yet I still felt far from God. Then I learned how to gain that two-handed grasp on God (by PLANTing and WATERing). I desired to "hear from God" like others. It was when someone explained to me how to keep in step with God's Spirit that my life began to move forward at light speed. This simple concept revolutionized my life.

Since we live by the Spirit, let us keep in
step with the Spirit.—GALATIANS 5:25

As you and God walk together, things are good and you feel at peace. Then temptation tries to get you to step in another direction. At that point, the Holy Spirit will whisper to you, "That is not good for you. Don't go there." If you agree and stay on track, you stay in step with the Spirit. When you give in to temptation, the Spirit whispers, "What you did is not a good choice. That is sin. Stop and take a spiritual breath." At this point you can exhale (agree with God and confess your error) and inhale (surrender to the Spirit's lead and ask him to fill or empower you),[1] which puts you back in step with him.

God commands us to "be filled with
the Spirit" (Ephesians 5:18).

As I practiced this simple process of staying in step, I saw my life change. I gained courage and confidence as I saw the fruit of the Spirit in my life: "But the fruit of the Spirit is love, joy, peace, forbearance, kindness, goodness, faithfulness, gentleness and self-control" (Galatians 5:22-23).

Now would be a great time to stop and talk to God. Pray and tell him you want to surrender to his leadership and that you want to be filled or empowered to live life through his power and not your own.

SAY YES!

Some of the best decisions I (Pam) have made can be traced back to what I call "listening to the whisper of God" (Romans 8:14-16). The whisper isn't an audible voice but an inner push toward healthy decisions.

I was eight when I first heard the Spirit whisper to my heart that God loved me and wanted a relationship with me. I was eighteen when I heard the Spirit whisper:

- "You need to make better choices in whom and how you date," so I decided not to date anyone who didn't share my faith in Jesus.

- "Go for it!" when my friend Grace invited me to join a Bible study on campus. It was there I met a mentor who helped me remake my life from the inside out.

- "*Read* God's Word daily and *do* what it says, no matter if you feel afraid."

- "*Go* to that leadership conference. See that guy across the lobby? *Talk to him*."
- "*Share* your new faith every day with someone."

I was twenty when I heard the Spirit whisper:

- "Spend the summer at a Bible institute."
- "Pam, I am calling you into ministry."
- "Say *yes*, Pam, when Bill proposes."

Every time I said yes to God's Spirit, my life took a turn upward.[2]

 Ask friends and family, "When was a time you said yes to God, and what was the outcome?"

Don't Be This Guy

Sam should have remarkable influence on everyone he meets. He is energetic, charismatic, confident, and personable. He has a way of raising the energy level in the room just by showing up which makes people think he will be a good friend who would be loyal, interested, and reliable.

When you get to know him, however, you realize he consistently makes poor decisions. The reality of who he is does not match what he appears to be. He qualified for financial aid from both the federal government and from an athletic scholarship. Rather than use it for rent, educational costs, and other living expenses, he bought drugs, paid for entertainment for himself and his friends, and bought toys to amuse himself. His roommates tried without success to get him to wake up in time to attend classes. They begged him to pay his rent, and then just grew angry with him before finally asking him to move out. He came back to his friends to apologize for his actions. They were all impressed until they realized he stole money from them before he left their house. It's hard to believe when you consider one of his former roommates was a local policeman.

> "A leader's most powerful ally is his
> or her own example."—JOHN WOODEN

Needless to say, they are disillusioned with him. He could have been a very significant part of their circle of friends. Instead, he has become an example of what none of them want to be.

STATEMENTS THAT SOUND
SMART BUT AREN'T

* *It won't be that bad because God will forgive us.*
  Although it's true that Jesus died to forgive all our sins (Psalm 103:12), anyone who uses God's gift of grace

to justify sin has not grasped the power of Christian living. It's like saying, "It's okay if I drive on the wrong side of the road because I am forgiven." That may be true, but who in their right mind wants to do it?

- *God wants me to be happy.* We don't disagree, but happiness without holiness is cruel. It might make you happy to eat chocolate for every meal, but it will ruin your health (Philippians 4:8-9).

- *It isn't loving to judge other people.* It's true that we aren't supposed to judge others when it comes to their value and their eternal state. When it comes to social behavior, however, we must judge one another's actions. Failure to do so would cause us all to live in chaos (Romans 13:1-6).

- *Religion has no place in political decisions.* Every political decision is a moral decision. Whether it involves money, education, authority, or social issues, every law reflects the morals of our society and the individuals who make these decisions. Everyone's morals are affected by their religious convictions, so you can never remove personal faith from public policy (Romans 13:1-6).

- *Faith does not need reasons to believe.* If you are willing to believe in something that doesn't make sense, you have real problems. We should commit only to principles that make sense. Certainly some

beliefs are bigger than we are, and we can't confirm
them like we can gravity or the need for oxygen. But
the bigger thoughts should be the logical conclusion
of smaller thoughts that can be verified. For instance,
we believe Jesus can give us eternal life as a gift
because he rose from the dead (1 Peter 3:15).

- *Anger makes me strong.* While it is true that righ-
teous anger can motivate us to do what is necessary
in the short-term (consider Jesus and the money
changers in the temple—Matthew 21:12-13), long-
term anger will produce bitterness, which will con-
sume our life and defile others (Hebrews 12:15).

Be Real About Your Dark Side

Part of being real means accepting that you have
a dark side to your soul. Sam Rima and Gary MacIn-
tosh, authors of *Overcoming the Dark Side of Leadership,*
assert that each of us has a tendency within us that is not
good, and can ruin your life. Look at the list below and
ask yourself, "Which of these am I most vulnerable to?"

- *Compulsive.* Some people are overly status con-
scious and need to be in authority. At their
core they are insecure, so they seek approval
from others, lean toward controlling behaviors
and are often workaholics. They can also be

moralistic or judgmental. Deep down, they feel life is out of control, so they need to control it.

- *Narcissistic.* Some people truly believe life revolves around them and their needs. They are driven to succeed by a need for admiration or acclaim. They have an overly inflated sense of the importance of their accomplishments, fantasies, and ideas. Deep down, they feel insecure and inferior, so they need to build themselves up.

- *Paranoid.* Fears stop some people from living a normal life. They are suspicious, jealous, fearful, and hypersensitive to the actions of others. They attach subjective meanings to others' motives and can create rigid structures to maintain control of situations or people. Deep down, these people are afraid of life or love.

- *Codependent.* Some people seek approval from a toxic person or live life around another's needs to the detriment of their own well-being. They seem like peacemakers because they don't want to confront real issues but would rather cover them up. They take on other's work and burdens and can have too high a tolerance for sin in others. Deep down, codependent people are repressed and frustrated because they never voice their true feelings or thoughts.

- *Passive-Aggressive.* Some people establish one expectation and then do the opposite. They complain, resist, and procrastinate as a means of controlling those around them. They can also occasionally use a small burst of depression or anger to control. Deep down, they are angry and bitter and fear success because others would raise expectations on them.

> "You may have to fight a battle more than once to win it."—MARGARET THATCHER

One way to minimize any of the above weaknesses is to focus on God's strength that is the opposite of your struggle. You can overcome your dark side by focusing on God's bright side.

Select the "dark side" trait you are most susceptible to, and then focus on the trait of God that can help you battle this weakness:

My Dark Side	God's Light
Compulsive	God's freedom, grace, mercy
Narcissistic	God as King, Ruler, Lord
Paranoid	God's provision, protection, peace
Codependent	God dependence, God pleaser, serving God

Passive-aggressive   God's path and plan
                        as priority

I believe my dark-side weakness might be

_____.

One thing I can do to address this weakness

is _____.[3]

Back on Track

Part of being real is a commitment to make course corrections along the way just as a GPS will tell you, "Turn around when possible," after you miss a turn or get off track. Second Peter 2:22 describes a person who doesn't take repentance seriously as "a dog [who] returns to its vomit," and "a sow that is washed [who] returns to her wallowing in the mud." It sounds gross, but it's a graphic picture of people who reveal their true character by their refusal to repent.

You might have to be tough on yourself to break the cycle of sin, but it is well worth it:

- *Talk*: Confess your sin, first to God, and then to a pastor, counselor, or leader who can walk you into freedom.

- *Walk*: Get away from those who want to drag you into sin. Break up any romantic relationship if the person you are dating wants you to violate a standard that you know in your heart is God's desire for you. Don't let emotional attraction today create emotional agony for the rest of your life.

- *Dock*: Just like you dock your iPod or iPhone to recharge, develop a regular schedule of church involvement and small group participation with authentic believers.

- *Block*: Get rid of anything that tempts you. Dump the drugs, bag the booze, purge the porn, cancel the cell numbers or texts of those who would lure you away from Christ's best.

- *Rock*: Commit to living "all out, all in" for Jesus and surround yourself with others who want that for themselves.

> "Do the best you can in every task, no matter how unimportant it may seem at the time."—SANDRA DAY O'CONNOR

Decide that you will be a person of integrity. Learn to energize the power of the Spirit in your life so you become the kind of person others can trust.

You Live

Choose one change or choice to make from this chapter and "sticky note" it on your mirror or on the desktop of your computer as a reminder to do it daily. Stay real.

 Go to www.Love-Wise.com/gradplus for some creative quiet times with God ideas.

@Jesus
"Greater love has no one than this: to lay down one's life for one's friends."

@Eleanor Roosevelt
"Understanding is a two-way street."

@Steven Covey
"Seek first to understand, then to be understood."

@Ralph Waldo Emerson
"We find in life exactly what we put into it."

Chapter 6

Decide to
Build a Network

Have you looked at a spider web recently? Close up? The spider works hard to build the web with strings of connection going out in a multitude of directions. Each string is small, but when they're connected together, they form a strong and effective network. Once the net is built, the spider generally hangs out in the center waiting to see what opportunities his web will bring.

You are like that spider. You live in a world of opportunity. There is so much, in fact, that you could never be involved with all of it, but if you have an effective network, you can attract some of it to your life with satisfying results.

The Solid Bridge

When a spider wants to spin a web, she first climbs to a high point. She then releases a heavy strand of silk into the air and lets the wind carry it out into her world. When she senses it has attached to something, she pulls in the slack and anchors it to the place where she has climbed. This forms the bridge she will attach the rest of the web to. It is the heaviest strand of silk she will use, and it will stay in place even when she takes down the rest of the web to rebuild it. It is the strand that holds the rest of the network together.

The bridge for you represents the most important relationship in your life. This is the person who

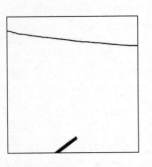 gives you more strength, more confidence, and more peace than anyone else. You will regularly check in with this person to make sure your life is going well and is on track. We believe the best candidate to be the bridge is Jesus. The

Bible describes him as the Savior, a rock, the light of the world, the prince of peace, God of all comfort, a refuge from the storm, a friend who sticks closer than a brother, and we could go on. He is simply the most

capable and committed person you will ever meet, so it makes sense to make your relationship with him your first priority.

Others will choose to make their most important relationship a family member, a close friend, a spouse, or even themselves. Even though none of these people are as strong as Jesus, we admit they can be effective in helping a person build his or her network.

The Sturdy Border

Once the bridge is established, the spider forms a border on which to attach her web. These outer strands are thicker than the ones she will use on the interior because they must support the rest of the network. She can handle damage to the interior strands, but when

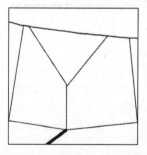

these outer ones get severed, the web collapses. She invests more into these to keep them strong and securely attached.

For you, the border represents your family and your vital friendships. These are the relationships in your network that provide personal stability, practical support, and a place to go to when things get rough.

"We should give our lives away first to those who
will cry at our funeral."—**PATRICK MORLEY**

Family First. Bill would be on that list for me (Pam).
He's a strong, independent man, but I know he would
be a mess if something unfortunate happened to me.
My three sons would look very strong, but I know they
would miss me. My mom, my brother, my sister, and
my sisters-in-law would console each other. In addition,
there is a short list of friends who know me extremely
well and are just as forgiving of my shortcomings as
they are supportive of my strengths.

Who is on your "short list"? Who are the
people you know for sure would be crying
at your funeral? How can you build into these relationships?

We know these close relationships have their ups
and downs, even though they form the main structure
of our networks. Regardless of how you might feel right
now, be assured that your parents love and care for you
more than anyone else alive. As a young adult, you have
probably experienced some chafing between you and
your parents. It's natural to feel rubbed the wrong way
at times as you launch. You're trying to take ownership of your own life while they're struggling to redefine
their role. It's hard on both sides when you're making

decisions that might need to be funded by their bank account. Do your best to remember, if Mom and Dad are still cutting you a check, they still have some say in how you run your business.

> "To understand the things that are at our door is the best preparation for understanding those things that lie beyond."—HYPATIA

PARENTS. WHAT IS GOING ON WITH THEM?

You may feel at times that your parents are unreasonable, over-involved, or unresponsive to your wishes and desires. You might even think they are a little over-emotional. When I (Pam) was adjusting to the graduation date of my oldest, I kept marking Brock's "lasts." I'd say things like, "This might be the last football game I'll ever see you play." "This might be the last Thanksgiving we're all together as a family, so will you say grace?" It turned out that I got to see him play other games, and we have celebrated numerous family holidays since, but it all felt drastic to me. Moms can be that way. (Sorry!)

Your parents' hearts and minds do somersaults as you launch from high school to college. At high school graduation, fear runs through a parent's heart and floods the mind with questions:

- Have I taught all that is needed to survive?

- Can we afford this next step?

- Will my graduate make good choices on her own?

- Will a major mistake derail his life plan?

- What will my life be like without my grad in it every day?

- Will my marriage, checkbook, and heart survive this stage of life?

These questions are ones your parents need to answer, but your patience with the process will keep them connected to your life.

A Strong Foundation

Any time you can answer your parents' questions *before* they ask them is a huge bonus for you. It will raise their confidence level in you and make every conversation easier. One way to do this is to download our "Freshman Foundation Dinner and Dialogue Questions" at www.Love-Wise.com. Then set up five meetings to talk through the core issues of taking over ownership of your life in five critical areas: fitness, finances, friendships, foundations, and future plans.

Our oldest asked us to join him on five walks along

the beach for five nights in a row at a family conference at Cannon Beach, Oregon. Son number two invited us to five dinners over a five-week period shortly after high school graduation. Our youngest son tackled one topic a month during the five months leading up to his graduation.

Keep in mind that legally, after eighteen, you are fully responsible for *all* of your life. Any help you get from parents, stepparents, grandparents, or anyone else is completely out of the goodness of their heart. Your job then is to appreciate their sacrifice and do well in that training.

In our family, we have a "scholarship" but it comes with requirements like any other scholarship program. Surprise your parents and bring the scholarship form and the "Freshman Foundation Questions" to *them*. Believe us, parents are more willing to part with their hard-earned money when their son or daughter is more responsible than the average student. (Download "Freshman Foundation" and "Scholarship Plan" samples at www.Love-Wise.com/gradplus.)

> Focus on what you do have, not what you don't.
> Focus on what the person you love can give,
> not what you expect or want them to give.

The Stable Middle

The third step in building a web is to create a stable internal structure. Once the spider has established borders that are strong, she adds internal threads to form a strategic network.

In your life, these represent the circle of friends and strategic contacts you develop upon which you will build your career and your influence. These are impor-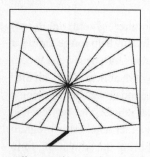tant relationships, but they are affected when you move, change the focus of your education or career, or progress to the next stage of your life.

As a graduate, you have a web or network of key relationships that will provide insight and wisdom for your decisions. The Bible says there is victory in a multitude of advisers (Proverbs 24:6). Because this group of people is so valuable to your future, we'll call this your "successnet." Who are some of these key players and why do you need them in your life?

You Gotta Have Friends

Friends are key players in your successnet. Your friendship circle is a great source of energy, encouragement, and enjoyment. So how do you find good, like-minded friends who share similar interests and values? A few ideas are: church, clubs, work, mutual interests and hobbies and volunteering. (Go to www.Love-Wise.com/gradplus for a more complete list of *Great Places to Meet Great Friends*.)

Could You Use a Little Advice?

You will face some intense decision points in your journey when you will want trusted people to help you discern your best course of action. Some mentors you'll want as a part of your successnet are:

Clergy. A pastor, college or youth pastor, director of women's or men's ministry, chaplains, parachurch or campus staff workers, or professors are some possibilities for mentors.

Caring leaders. Student small-group or Bible study leaders, upperclassmen or club leaders, business leaders, older women or men in your church, or mature Christians you meet during your college or early career years can provide guidance.

Counselors. If you've experienced trauma or are lugging around emotional baggage from your past, it can be well worth the time, effort, and cost to interact with a counselor to rebuild the affected areas of your life.

> "No matter what accomplishments you make,
> somebody helps you."—WILMA RANDOLPH

Expand the Net

In your late teens and early twenties, you'll want

to methodically take ownership of your life. These are some other professionals you will want to get to know:

- Health-care professionals
- Insurance agent
- Financial advisor
- Lawyer or legal help
- Automobile dealer and mechanic
- Realtor/mortgage broker
- Contractor/home maintenance person

Tips on how to find quality professionals to connect with can be found at www.Love-Wise.com/gradplus.

Have you identified all or most of the key people needed for your successnet? If you haven't, talk about which relationships need to be built and how you'll go about making those new connections.

The Sticky Center

The final step in building a web is to create a sticky center that catches opportunity. After the internal structure has been established, the spider will work her way around the center of the web laying down a sticky spiral of silk to catch the bugs that will bring her nourishment.[1]

In your life, the sticky center represents interpersonal skills that cause others to want to spend time with

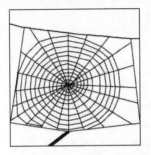

you and include you in their networks. The key to attracting opportunities that stick is trust. People won't listen to you unless they trust you. People won't hire you unless they trust you. People will not invest in further training for you unless they trust you. In simple terms, people will conclude you are trustworthy if you show them you can be trusted.

Twelve Tips to Connect with Others

Practicing the following skills when you are in a social setting, professional seminar, or business environment will help you garner success in strategic interpersonal relationships:

1. *Relax.* Remember that many in the room might be more uncomfortable than you are. Seek to be a blessing, to be other-centered, and to do what you can to help others feel welcome and at ease.

2. *Shake hands firmly.* Don't give a "vise grip" greeting because it will make people feel as though

you're trying to intimidate them. Look the person in the eye and smile. Express a simple, "So nice to meet you."

3. *Ask God to lead you to the people he wants you to meet.* Ask God for wisdom to discern if you are supposed to listen, serve, encourage, or instruct the ones you meet.

4. *Mirror what others are doing.* If everyone is talking quietly, talk quietly. If others are eating, have a snack. If you don't know what to do, look to see what others are doing and do it. Look at the art, the view, the book table. But *never* feel the need to break your moral convictions whether it involves alcohol, language, or other behaviors. People will respect you if you simply say, "Thanks but no thanks. That's just not my thing." And if they don't respect you, that's your cue that this group is not for you.

5. *Be a good listener.* People will perceive you as a successful, interesting, outgoing person if you are just nice. Listen attentively so if others lose their place in the conversation, you can gently help them get back on track.

6. *Have a few prepared questions to avoid awkward silences.* Usually the obvious questions work well: "What brought you here?" "Tell me a

little about yourself." "If you weren't here today, what would you like to be doing?"

7. *Compliment others.* Describe how you were affected by something they said or an opinion they shared. If nothing comes to mind, compliment something they're wearing or something they've said they enjoy doing.

8. *Dig a little.* Comments such as, "That's interesting—tell me more," "I'd love to hear more of your thoughts about…" or "How insightful; give me your opinion on…" draw people to you. Just be careful not to interrogate like a police detective.

9. *Do a little research.* If you know some of the people who might be at the event, Google them or go to their Facebook pages, blogs, or web pages. We did say do a *little* research. If you come with too much information or start a conversation with, "I googled you," chances are the conversation isn't going to go well. Simply look for the facts that will help you ask meaningful and interesting questions.

10. *Watch for nonverbal cues.* One study at UCLA indicated that up to 93 percent of communication effectiveness is determined by nonverbal cues.[2] If the person you're talking with checks

his or her watch or keeps looking past you to others, take the hint. Excuse yourself to use the restroom or say, "It's been so nice talking to you. I really should excuse myself. I see an old friend across the room I should greet."

11. *Have a good joke.* Humor sets people at ease. In a survey we supervised of what the opposite gender finds attractive, humor is number two on the list, just behind "Person of growing faith in God." Humor is ranked even higher than "Has a job."

12. *Tell a good story.* Learn from others. Listen to the kind of stories others share. We all have interesting lives, but few of us think to pay attention to the stories so we can tell them later. As you work, meet new people, interact with friends, and travel, look for stories that match the goal of Universal Studios: "To Make People Laugh, Cry or Sit on the Edge of Their Chairs."[3] Chances are if you enjoyed a story, others will also. The key is to tell the story as succinctly as possible and get to the punch line quickly. If you ramble, people will wander.

What interpersonal relationship skill did you learn or were you reminded of that if you applied it, would make the biggest positive change in your life?

Protect the Network

Once you include someone in your network, treat them, their contacts, resources, and friends as fine china or crystal that can easily be broken. If someone is complimentary to you, do not assume you have permission to post their words on Facebook or on your blog. People own their words, so ask permission to make them public before you post them. Here are a few principles for people protecting:

Be grateful. If someone offers assistance or resources to you, thank them for offering and then be patient with the timing. We are mentors to many, and are naturally drawn to the ones who have an appreciative spirit. We lose motivation when they are pushy or demanding. The faster you realize that the world doesn't owe you a living, the quicker others will be to offer you opportunities.

People own their kindness, so it's within their right to choose the timing for when they give it away to you.

Be discreet. Another aspect of protecting your successnet of relationships is to respect others' privacy and represent yourself authentically. Just because you talked with someone once doesn't mean you are his or her best friend. So don't represent yourself as something you are not.

Be prompt. Honor others' time. If you make an appointment, arrive early. If the person you're meeting runs late, give him or her grace. The more important someone is, the longer you should be willing to wait for them to give you their time. Always thank someone for their time. If your appointment time is coming to a close and you still have questions or items to discuss, ask the other person if you can have a specific number of extra minutes of their time. If that's not possible, ask if you can make a follow-up appointment. If you have respected the time they've given you, they are more likely to give you more.

> Time is the most valuable resource on earth
> because you can never get it back.

Be prepared. Felicia Alvarez is a motivated young lady. I (Pam) consider it a privilege to be mentoring her in her writing, leading, and speaking skills because she always comes well prepared. She emails any paperwork I might need to review ahead of time. She brings two hard copies (one for each of us) of her work and a list of questions she wants to ask so that our time is used effectively. When I challenge her, offer a correction to help her grow, or give her homework, she receives it willingly and thanks me rather than being defensive or argumentative. She expresses her gratefulness for my time, goes above and beyond on any assignment or task I ask of her, and sends thank you notes. When I look at my limited schedule and all the people who want my time, Felicia is at the top of my list.

The best leaders are first great followers.

You Live

Make a list of ten people who have the character you want, who have accomplished the goals you dream of, who have relationships like the ones you desire, and who have integrity you can look up to. Pray, and respond when God provides opportunities for you to meet them in person. Introduce yourself and offer to serve in their world to learn from them.

 Go to www.Love-Wise.com/gradplus and gain more advice from mentors.

@Helen Keller
"Walking with a friend in the dark is better than walking alone in the light."

@Anne Morrow Lindbergh
"Good communication is as stimulating as black coffee, and just as hard to sleep after."

@William Arthur Ward
"When we seek to discover the best in others, we somehow bring out the best in ourselves."

@Cicero
"Friendship is love with wings."

@Miguel de Cervantes
"Tell me what company thou keepest, and I'll tell thee what thou art."

@Walter Winchell
"A friend is one who walks in when others walk out."

Chapter 7

Decide to Invest in Relationships

Relationships can be exciting, thrilling, exhilarating—and frustrating, annoying, heartbreaking, and very unpredictable at times. The decisions we make in our friendships, acquaintances, colleagues, and romantic interests change the course of our lives.

> You are either making healthy decisions
> and creating relationships that thrive or
> you are making unhealthy decisions that
> cause relationships to deteriorate.

Making investments in relationships begins with learning to define the level of involvement you are willing to have with each person in your life. Along your journey, you will engage in five different levels of connection. Each level represents an increase in trust, commitment, and vulnerability. If you pay attention to the intensity level of each friendship and make decisions that are in sync with the kind of relationship it really is, your interactions will be healthy at all levels.

It's Second Nature

The goal is to develop a second nature for characterizing your associations—relationship instincts, if you will. When you started driving, you were awkward, uncomfortable, and nervous, but you stayed at it. You're not exactly sure when it happened, but one day driving became a natural skill. At times, of course, you have to give intense focus to your driving because unexpected things happen on the road, but you accept that as an ordinary part of driving.

Relationships are the same way. The relational skills you need to learn can make you feel tense, awkward, and uncomfortable at first. As you practice the skills, your comfort level grows until the day it becomes second nature. As with driving, you encounter surprises and unexpected moves as your involvement grows, and these require intensified focus and effort. If your skills are well developed, you'll accept this as a normal part of your relationships, make the necessary adjustments, and get back on track.

Can You C What's Happening?

Every stage of involvement has corresponding levels of conversation, physical contact, and social commitments. When you operate within the appropriate boundaries, every association in your life can be healthy and valuable. When you wander outside these boundaries, any relationship can become uncomfortable and toxic to your personal growth. Consider the following relationship ladder:

RELATIONSHIP LADDER			
	Type of Relationship		
Level of Involvement	Friendships	Work Relationships	Romantic Interests
Cautious	Acquaintances	Acquaintances	Acquaintances
Curious	Casual Friends	Colleagues	Casual Dating
Confident	Trusted Friends	Trainees	Exclusive Dating
Connected	Mentors/ Parents/ Grandparents	Mentors	Fiancé/ Fiancée
Committed			Husband/ Wife

You can't tell at first if this
person is weird or wonderful.

Because of this, if you want to learn more about what to do at every level of relationship: cautious, curious, confident, connected, and committed—or if you want to see where a relationship is headed, or what level you are at with someone, go to www.Love-Wise.com/gradplus and learn more.

Relationships are matters of the heart and can change quickly, which is why defining them is so important. Our friend Arlene is a good example:

> When I was in high school, I was blessed to have a lot of titles. Cheerleader. Honors Student. Student Body President. But there was one title I was very displeased with—Dateless. I felt like I was the only one to graduate from my high school without being asked out.
>
> With a sense of anticipation, I began attending a Christian college where I thought for sure I would meet my match. After all, there were so many new, cute Christian boys everywhere. I didn't want to define my whole life by my dating status, so I pursued my education, new leadership roles, and ways of serving God. Four years later, I received my BA but alas, no MRS degree. But I did come close.
>
> During my senior year, I began dating a terrific young man. He was involved in youth group and studying to be in the ministry. He was kind, smart, quick to smile, captain of the volleyball team, and cute to boot. I thought beyond a shadow of a

doubt, *This is the Mr. Wonderful I've been waiting for all my life!*

One night, I felt terribly sad for no apparent reason. When I asked God why I was crying, I was drawn to the story of Abraham and Isaac. Was I willing to sacrifice my Isaac on the altar? Was I willing to let my relationship die? Would I be true to God even if I remained single? Tearfully, I said yes to God. A few days later, my boyfriend broke up with me. Just a few short weeks before, I was convinced he was the one, even though he turned out to be just a great friend along the journey. Boy, am I glad now that we didn't get any more involved with each other than we did.

You'll find your partner on your path of purpose.
Move toward your purpose, and let God
encourage the person to move toward you.

Because Arlene kept appropriate boundaries, she was free from nagging regrets and could focus on her future. She chose to attend graduate school to pursue a degree in media and communications where her Mr. Right was on his vocational path.

The first time I ever saw James, he was flipping hamburgers at a welcome barbeque at the graduate school we both attended. It wasn't love at first sight around the condiment bar, but he did catch my eye. We became good friends and before long it became clear to me that he was *the one*. Unfortunately, it took him longer to catch this revelation.

After months of being only good friends, I had to reevaluate my desire for James. Again, I surrendered my wishes to God. My theme verse was Psalm 37:4 (ESV), "Delight yourself in the LORD, and he will give you the desires of your heart." I prayed that God would either take away my desire for James, or place that same desire in his heart. A few months later, James asked me on our first date to Outback Steakhouse. Thank God he talked to a friend who discouraged him from taking me to Dairy Queen. At dessert, he pulled out a red rose and a yellow rose that he had discreetly hidden in his jacket. He said, "We've been friends for a long time (the yellow rose), and I want to date you and see if there's something more (the red rose)."

Defining the relationship freed James and Arlene to fall in love in a way that protected their hearts and built trust. Arlene adds, "It's been twelve years since I married Mr. Wonderful. Was he worth all those days of waiting in high school, college, and beyond? Without a doubt, *yes!*"

Choose Your Limits

You live in a world that treats sexual activity casually as if it has minor consequences. Don't be fooled. Your sexuality is both priceless and powerful. Treated with respect, sexual activity produces children, provides fun, promotes intimacy, reduces stress, and proclaims God's love to the world. Treated casually or carelessly, it can still produce children, but it adds fear to intimacy, frustration to our emotions, and a frantic sense of distrust.

> Sex is like dynamite: In marriage it can blow away fears and frustrations to build a life. Outside marriage, sex and the consequences can blow away hopes, dreams, and opportunities.

What Science Has to Say

Physicians Joe McIlhaney and Freda Bush report in *Hooked*, "When we do something exciting, dopamine rewards us by...making the brain cells produce a feeling of excitement or of well-being...it makes us feel the need or desire to repeat pleasurable, exciting, and rewarding acts."[1] And sex is one of the strongest generators of these aggressive pleasure creators.

"It should be noted, however," McIlhaney and Bush say, "that dopamine [and oxytocin] is values-neutral... [it]cannot tell right from wrong." The doctors report that all of us are just as "vulnerable to falling into a cycle of dopamine reward for unwise sexual behavior... The pattern of changing sex partners...seems to damage their ability to bond in a committed relationship."[2] This helps explain why some people keep dating a loser—or jumping from relationship to relationship—he or she has become addicted.

In addition, casual sex is becoming more risky as unwanted pregnancies, STDs, and the divorce rate keep increasing. (Go to www.Love-Wise.com/gradplus for a list of more risks of sex outside of marriage.)

In a world that ignores the risks and encourages you to hook up, have "friends with benefits," make sex part of dating relationships, engage in intimate contact with a multitude of partners, utilize sexting and pornography, how can you determine what is truly healthy when it comes to your sexual choices?

Fortunately, God has spoken clearly on the issue. The Bible never says we should avoid sex, but 1 Thessalonians 4:3 explicitly says it is God's will for us to "avoid sexual immorality." God commands us to draw a hard line prior to sexual intercourse in our romantic activity before marriage. (And by sexual intercourse we mean all forms of intimate sex, including oral sex or the foreplay that leads to intercourse.)

The discussion doesn't stop there, however. In the beatitudes, Jesus said, "Blessed are the pure in heart, for they will see God" (Matthew 5:8). The goal in our sexual lives is to operate with a pure heart. When we do, we can be unashamed, unapologetic, and later in marriage, unreserved and uninhibited.

We encourage you to picture your sexual choices on a continuum. At one end is holding hands, while sexual intercourse is at the other end. Ask yourself, "Where do I need to set the line for each relationship level to maintain a pure heart?" You will save yourself a lot of turmoil and enhance your most valuable relationships if you deliberately decide *ahead of time* the appropriate physical contact for each type of relationship in your life.

> Pay now with self-discipline, or pay later
> the consequences of life's discipline.

GIVING UP OUR POWER—
GAINING HEAVEN'S PROVIDENCE

The Spirit will challenge you to go against the cultural norms and take a higher path to harness the power of your passions. Brock and Hannah met because her parents owned a Christian bookstore where I (Pam) did a book signing. As "concerned moms," we passed along contact information to our children who happened to both be students at Liberty University. They decided to take the risk to meet and...

> Our friendship quickly blossomed into dating,
> even though we both wanted to be cautious. We
> had been in serious relationships in the past that
> hadn't worked out very well, so we decided to
> be deliberate about our relationship. On our
> second date, Brock and I talked about our families and what we wanted to be when we grew up.

Then the conversation turned to us as a couple. I was impressed when Brock said he respected me and didn't want to do anything that would cause me not to respect him. Based on that, he said he wouldn't kiss me. He knew that just one kiss would be a step in the wrong direction for him. It would cause us to focus on the physical side of our relationship rather than more important issues like spiritual convictions, life goals, and personal ethics.

Because we limited physical affection to holding hands, we were able to talk, pray, and laugh without the pressure that other couples face. That same night we also decided we wouldn't be alone in a house. We could go in only if someone else was present.

In addition to setting up safeguards, we agreed to pray together every night before we went to our separate dorms. Our friendship quickly intensified. It didn't take too long before we knew that we wanted to be together forever. After dating for one year, Brock asked my dad if he could marry me. When Brock proposed, we kissed for the first time. Our wedding day was filled with pure, beautiful joy because we knew that we had saved ourselves for each other.

You Live

Do you need to make any changes in the way you relate to any friends? Are you giving away too much of yourself without asking for a rising level of commitment?

Select someone you respect to be a sounding board as you talk through your friendships and dating life. Are there any changes that need to happen at any level of your relationships?

 Go to www.Love-Wise.com/gradplus to download your own chart and decide now your boundaries that will protect your future. Consider buying a copy of our book, *Single Men Are Like Waffles—Single Women Are Like Spaghetti* and focus on honing your relationship skills to create a life and a love to look forward to.

@Viola Ruelke Gommer
"As you walk along the path before you, it may seem strange and new. You are not alone. The One who made you watches over you and guides your feet. He knows the way."

@Margaret Chase Smith
"The right way is not always the popular and easy way. Standing for right when it is unpopular is a true test of moral character."

Chapter 8

Decide to Be
on God's Team

s a coed cheerleader, our son Zach could hold
girls over his head in precarious positions,
sometimes as he was standing on the shoulders of another male teammate. Once, while he was
holding his partner over his head, I (Pam) asked her,
"Aren't you afraid? One false move and you could be
dead. Aren't you afraid he'll drop you?"

"Not at all," she said. "Zach would never drop me.
He'd risk his own life to save mine."

While Zach is committed to lay down his life if necessary to save his partner, still he is human and fallible.
God is 100 percent sure, 100 percent reliable, 100 percent accurate. He is a sure and steady partner—and he
desires to team with you.

God is looking for partners in life—he's looking to uphold you to secure your success. "For the eyes of the LORD range throughout the earth to strengthen those whose hearts are fully committed to him" (2 Chronicles 16:9).

God's on Your Team

Consider all the things God has done to show you his love, just because he wanted to:

- He gave you a heart to know him. "I will give them a heart to know me, that I am the LORD. They will be my people, and I will be their God" (Jeremiah 24:7).

- He made himself easy to find. "You will seek me and find me when you seek me with all your heart" (Jeremiah 29:13).

- He wrote his law on your heart. That means an understanding of what is right and wrong is written inside you to guide your decisions. "I will put my law in their minds and write it on their hearts. I will be their God, and they will be my people" (Jeremiah 31:33).

- He placed his Holy Spirit in you as a guarantee that he will give you eternal life and everything that goes with it. "He anointed us, set his seal of ownership on us, and put his Spirit in our hearts as a deposit, guaranteeing what is to come" (2 Corinthians 1:21-22).

- He wants you to call him Daddy. "Because you are his sons, God sent the Spirit of his Son into our hearts, the Spirit who calls out, '*Abba*, Father'" (Galatians 4:6). *Abba* is the equivalent of *daddy* or *papa* in Aramaic.

God has already committed himself to you. Now it's your turn. As you seek him with all your heart, he will make you stronger than you ever imagined.

God's Teammates Put Their Talents into Action

You have probably figured out by now that you are a talented, intelligent, and uniquely gifted person. Developing your gifts starts with hard work. This is where the partnership with God comes into play. Your talents reside within you, but they do not operate smoothly until you put in the hours of effort required to develop them.

The same is true with more advanced skills such as music, teaching, athletics, technology, and leadership. To create sufficient "muscle memory" to function at a high level, you must put in hundreds of hours of practice and repetition. Author and speaker Bill Butterworth says that what distinguishes excellent violinists from average or mediocre violinists is not talent; it's ten thousand hours of practice.[1] Practice does make perfect. John Wooden, one of basketball's most successful coaches, said, "The best competition I have is against myself to become better." That's the attitude of someone who wants to partner well with God. God gives his best, and we give back our desire to be empowered by him to give our best.

> "As for other matters, brothers and sisters, we instructed you how to live in order to please God, as in fact you are living. Now we ask you and urge you in the Lord Jesus to do this more and more."—1 THESSALONIANS 4:1

God wants you to actively develop your talents because he created you as an original. There never has been and never will be anyone exactly like you.

"Before I formed you in the womb I knew you, before you were born I set you apart; I appointed you as a prophet to the nations" (Jeremiah 1:5).

For you created my inmost being; you knit me together in my mother's womb. I praise you because I am fearfully and wonderfully made… Your eyes saw my unformed body; all the days ordained for me were written in your book before one of them came to be (Psalm 139:13-16).

Discovering your uniqueness is not like reading a recipe where everything is spelled out in detail. It is more like a treasure hunt or a forensics investigation. It requires you to be inquisitive. Some of the questions you can ask to discover your unique strengths, calling, and passion are below:

1. What do you love?

2. What do you do better than the average person?

3. What do you not do well? What do you not enjoy? (It's just as important to know what to say no to as what to say yes to.)

4. What compliments do people give you regularly?

5. Make a list of five or six times when you did something for others and you felt God's approval or encouragement. (Maybe you thought, *Wow, that went well* or *Awesome, that was fun. I think I helped someone out.*)

6. If you were guaranteed success and had all the time, money, and resources needed, what would you want to do for God or to make the world a better place?

7. When you are all alone and it's quiet, where do your thoughts and daydreams take you?

8. What issues in the news make you say, "That just isn't right. Someone should do something about that."

9. What beliefs or values would you be willing to go public to defend?

10. What do you talk about the most? (Where your mouth is, there your heart is also.)[2]

Look over your answers for repeating words. If you used the word *listen* a lot, you probably have higher than average empathy and may be heading for a career in counseling, the medical field, or ministry. If you notice the repeated use of *led* or *lead*, you're most likely headed toward some kind of decision-making or people-motivating position. If you use words such as *create, build,* or *invent,* you'll do well to consider a future in engineering, manufacturing, or construction. (For more information on discovering your unique bent, you can pick up *Woman of Influence, The 10 Best Decisions a Woman Can Make,* or *The 10 Best Decisions a Man Can Make.* We also recommend you work through career assessment inventories, such as *Career Direct Assessment* from Crown Financial Ministries, which surveys your talents, skills, passions, work environment preferences, and values.[1])

Gather friends and family you trust and share the answers to the above questions. Ask this group to give their feedback and pray with you. Some questions you might ask are:

- What strengths do you see in me?

- What do you think is unique about me?

> "Do first that which only you
> can do."—DAISY HEPBURN

God's Teammates Show Up

Teammates show up for both the good days and the bad days. They show up for rehearsal as well as the performance. They are as committed to practice as they are to the game. In the midst of the boring and the beautiful moments of life, God's teammates realize "it is God who works in you to will and to act in order to fulfill his good purpose" (Philippians 2:13). They are, therefore, motivated to "do everything without grumbling or arguing, so that you may become blameless and pure, children of God without fault in a warped and crooked generation" (2:14-15).

> "Do the best you can in every task, no
> matter how unimportant it may seem at
> the time."—SANDRA DAY O'CONNOR

Hannah had to wrestle with this attitude to decide if she really wanted to be on God's team.

I grew up taking Jesus for granted. I went to a Christian school, attended church every Sunday, mastered AWANA, and excelled in VBS. I asked Christ into my life when I was young and grew up in a Christian home, but I was lacking the joy of Christianity. By the time I reached high school, I strongly disliked church. I didn't like the people, the building, the air around it, or even the landscaping (okay, I may be overstating it, but I had certainly lost interest). By the end of my junior year, my parents had grown tired of my attitude, so they decided to be proactive: they signed me up for a mission's trip to Guatemala.

It was a trip for upcoming seniors to develop leadership skills. Each of the students on the trip was responsible for a different aspect. The goal was to have an entirely student-led trip, so the adults were simply chaperones. Given that I didn't like anyone who was going, I was mad. I didn't want to lead. I didn't want to go to a foreign country. And I didn't want to hang out with this group. But I needed my parents to provide a place to live, food to eat, and clothes to wear, so I showed up for the first meeting.

Much to my surprise, I had fun. Who knew that if you actually spent time with people from church, you could have fun and find common ground? I was assigned the task of being the banker so I was in charge of all the money for gas, food, water, etc. while we were in Guatemala. If I didn't plan appropriately, everyone would be affected. If the girl in charge of the menu didn't know the food budget, she might plan meals that were too expensive. I had to coordinate closely with the guy in charge of getting clean, bottled water or we would all be in trouble. It was my first experience in working as a team. We became unified as we worked together building an orphanage and studying the Old Testament book of Nehemiah.

God opened my eyes to the potential of being a part of God's team through that trip. Based on my experience, I decided to make my life verse, "Whatever happens, conduct yourselves in a manner worthy of the gospel of Christ" (Philippians 1:27).

> "Only God can satisfy the hungry
> heart."—HUGH BLACK

Run like a Winner

In trying to get his friends to grasp this vital truth, Paul compared life to athletic competition.

> Do you not know that in a race all the runners run, but only one gets the prize? Run in such a way as to get the prize...Therefore I do not run like someone running aimlessly; I do not fight like a boxer beating the air. No, I strike a blow to my body and make it my slave so that after I have preached to others, I myself will not be disqualified for the prize (1 Corinthians 9:24-27).

Paul entered the race of life as a talented competitor who trained to win. He exercised self-discipline so he wouldn't miss out on the prize God made available to him. The inconsistency in our souls requires a strong dose of self-discipline if we're to realize our unique contribution.

The Workout Plan

Step 1: Capture your thoughts. Second Corinthians 10:5 says, "we take captive every thought to make it obedient to Christ." The picture here is of binding our thoughts in chains, much as someone taken prisoner would be bound, so they obey us rather than running wild. In practical terms this means we ask, "Is this thought true?" If it is, we let it run and we follow it enthusiastically. If it's not, we aggressively declare it to be wrong and refuse to follow its lead.

Step 2: Create habits. We need to practice those things that encourage our hearts to focus on what is good. (Remember PLANT and WATER?) The heart gets attached to what it is exposed to the most, so we can form strong attachments to what is true with these simple disciplines.

Step 3: Confirm it's working. The best way to confirm the value of a skill is to teach it to someone else. Helping others live well forces you to clarify what you actually believe.

Pride brings a person low, but the lowly in
spirit gain honor.—PROVERBS 29:23

It May Not Be Fair but It's the Way It Is

When character is lacking, opportunities become limited very fast. Just recently we heard a coach from a Pac-12 school describe the way their graduate assistants comb their recruits' Facebook pages. They recently dropped two promising recruits because of inappropriate remarks and posts. The sad thing is that some of the remarks were made by people these recruits associated with rather than by the recruits themselves.

Some of you are thinking, *That's not fair*. You're right, it isn't fair. But it's the way it is. Today, the best of who you are and the worst of who you are can be broadcast for all to see in less time than it takes you to ask, "Is this a good idea?" If you're not careful, your sins will find you out, and nowadays they will find you out seriously fast. Select a simple verse as your inner compass like, "Love must be sincere. Hate what is evil; cling to what is good" (Romans 12:9) or "Bad company corrupts good character" (1 Corinthians 15:33).

> "Your reputation is what you are perceived to be. Your character is what you really are."—JOHN WOODEN

God's Teammates Follow the Playbook

A musician follows a musical score, a programmer follows detailed computer code, and an athlete studies and lives out his playbook. God has a playbook for your life too because life is an intricate journey. It is easy to get overwhelmed by the myriad of choices in life so God provided his guidance to walk you through to your success.

> "God asks no one whether he will accept life. That is not a choice. You must take it. The only choice is how."—HENRY WARD BEECHER

Abraham's servant must have felt this way when he was assigned this tough job: "Go to my country and my own relatives and get a wife for my son Isaac" (Genesis 24:4). Can you imagine? "Hey Bill, you know I love my son more than anyone else on earth. I have a problem that I want you to help me solve. We're living in a foreign land, and I don't want him to marry any of the women around here. I want you to go back to my homeland and find the perfect woman for my son to marry. And Bill, don't mess this up. This is my only son."

Where do you even start when you get an assignment that overwhelms you? How do you get your feet under you when you're asked to do something brand new for which you have no experience?

Abraham's servant had no experience in matchmaking, but he'd been given the responsibility. He got off to a wise start by asking the Lord to guide him to just the right person:

"LORD, God of my master Abraham, make me successful today, and show kindness to my master Abraham. See, I am standing beside this spring, and the daughters of the townspeople are coming out to draw water. May it be that when I say to a young woman, 'Please let down your jar that I may have a drink,' and she says, 'Drink, and I'll water your camels too'—let her be the one you have chosen for your servant Isaac. By this I will know that you have shown kindness to my master" (Genesis 24:12-14).

Later, when describing what had happened, he told Rebekah's brother Laban, "Before I finished praying in my heart, Rebekah came out, with her jar on her shoulder...and said, 'Drink, and I'll water your camels too'" (vv. 45-46). The plan had been conceived in the servant's heart, and the Lord confirmed it by answering his prayer.

> "We have a God who delights in
> impossibilities."—ANDREW MURRAY

The Championship

You no doubt have watched a football game where against all odds one team rallied for a comeback win, and the coach was drenched in ice-cold Gatorade. You've also probably seen a basketball team make a shot at the buzzer to pull out a victory and watched the cheering team lift a player up to cut down the net as a victory souvenir. The victory is especially sweet because it seemed supernatural.

When you have training and experience, it makes sense to rely on what you know works. But you'll face other times when you must accomplish what you've never done before. You'll need a miracle, you'll be praying for supernatural power, you'll be banking on God to come through in ways that will leave you amazed.

This is why it's so important for you to decide to be on God's team. You will be much more effective if you learn how to let him speak to your heart. You will choose better if you have access to his wisdom.

> "Without the Way, there is no going; without the Truth, there is no knowing; without the Life, there is no living."—**THOMAS À KEMPIS**

God is assembling a team to tell the world the greatest message of hope and strength that exists. He's looking for you.

> "I must have the drive to develop my abilities and become the best I can be so that I'll be ready. If I'm prepared, perhaps my chance will come. But if I am not primed, I'll miss my opportunity and it isn't likely to come again. I have to think as if I'm only going to get one shot, so I must be ready."—**JOHN WOODEN**

You Live

Have you made the smart, wise, intelligent, prudent, practical, sensible decision to be on God's team? It can be as simple as: "Flee the evil desires of youth and pursue righteousness, faith, love and peace, along with those who call on the Lord out of a pure heart" (2 Timothy 2:22). Call on God, call out to God. He wants you on his team.

 Go to www.Love-Wise.com/gradplus to learn more about being on God's team.

@Barbara Bush
"At the end of your life, you will never regret not having passed one more test, not winning one more verdict, not closing one more deal. You will regret time not spent with a husband, a child, a friend, a parent."

@Charles de Montesquieu
"To become truly great, one has to stand with people, not above them."

@Helen Nielsen
"Humility is like underwear; essential, but indecent if it shows."

@Benjamin Franklin
"Humility makes great men twice honorable."

Chapter 9

Decide to Serve Others

We all know at least one. A person full of himself—egotistical, arrogant, conceited. These people live well beyond appropriate confidence and have jumped on over to pompousness. When Answerbag posted the question, "Who is the most egotistical person you have ever met?" some interesting answers appeared:

- My dad, because he…cares for no one but himself. He thinks he's God's gift to the planet.

- My first ex. He thought he was gravity and everything revolved around him.

- My sister-in-law, we call her Godzilla. She thinks that she knows everything and is disgustingly nasty when she tells everyone.

- My cousin...whenever I go anywhere with him he uses my bad points to emphasize his good points.

- Myself, because I am totally absorbed in my own world. Practically everything I do is for the purpose of trying to make myself happy. Just being honest.[1]

You can tell from the descriptions that these people don't have much positive influence. If we aren't careful, pride can take over our lives as well.

What is Success?

Jesus redefined success:

"Whoever wants to become great among you must be your servant...just as the Son of Man did not come to be served, but to serve, and to give his life as a ransom for many" (Matthew 20:25-28).

You will find true success, lasting influence, and God-pleasing achievements on the path of servanthood. The greatest accomplishment in the history of the world was the death and resurrection of Christ. Nothing else has made it possible for everyone to be free, forgiven, and live forever. No company has produced more. No entrepreneur has invented more. No community leader has helped more people. And Jesus did it by being a servant who sacrificed for the sake of others.

Serving Others Leads to Greatness

Jesus didn't just instruct people to have the attitude of a servant, he lived it. One day after a long, hot, dirty walk, "he got up from the meal, took off his outer clothing, and wrapped a towel around his waist. After that, he poured water into a basin and began to wash his disciples' feet, drying them with the towel that was wrapped around him" (John 13:4-5).

Peter was so shook up by the sight he blurted out, "Lord, are you going to wash my feet?" (v. 6). It felt wrong. His rabbi should not be washing feet. The Messiah should not be doing such menial work. The Son of God should not be serving those he created.

Jesus simply replied, "You do not realize now what I am doing, but later you will understand" (v. 7). He was setting the tone for real influence. He was showing them how to impact people in a way that would last forever. He was demonstrating the ironic path to greatness.

> When he had finished washing their feet, he put on his clothes and returned to his place. "Now that I, your Lord and Teacher, have washed your feet, you also should wash one another's feet. I have set you an example that you should do as I have done for you" (vv. 12-17).

"A diploma is not a certificate of right to special favor and profit in the world but rather a commission to service."—**WARREN HARDING**

WHAT DOES IT LOOK LIKE TO BE A SERVANT?

- I will look for tasks that need to be done and do them *before* anyone asks me.

- I will seek to make the life of others easier, less stressful, less of a hassle.

- I will not draw attention to myself; rather I will draw attention to others.

- I will desire the best for others.

- I will look for ways to help others become successful.

- I will create a calm and nurturing environment.

- I will do work so those around me function in their unique strength.

- I will choose a "will do," "can do," "love to do" attitude.

- I will perform repetitive responsibilities as a privilege not a duty.

- I will choose manners and grace that can put others at ease.

- I will use words that express confidence in and respect for the people I serve.

> You, my brothers and sisters, were called
> to be free. But do not use your freedom to
> indulge the flesh; rather, serve one another
> humbly in love.—GALATIANS 5:13

Serving Others Leads to Confidence

Humility realizes God created you as competent and capable. You have talents and insights that match the purpose for which God shaped you (Psalm 139:13-18) as well as a spiritual gift empowered by the Holy Spirit for the good of others (1 Corinthians 12:7-11).

As a result, you should expect that you're going to perform quite well in these areas of your life. When you are confident in these areas, you are humbly accepting that God created you to serve with those capabilities. You cross over to pride when you start to think you somehow created the abilities you enjoy.

> "Humility is to make a right estimate of
> one's self."—CHARLES H. SPURGEON

In *Woman of Influence*, I (Pam) talk about my journey with pride: "I caught myself wondering how I could be guilty of pride since I battle a self-confidence problem so often. Then God pointed out that an oversensitive low self-esteem is pride inside out. When I battle low self-esteem, I am still focusing on me. God wants my eyes on him."[2]

Base your identity on who God says you are
and be committed to do nothing more and
nothing less than what your identity demands.

The Road to Humility

The path to humility is often comical:

God, in his infinite wisdom, knew that I (Brock) could easily become proud, so he made sure I drove vehicles during high school that would keep me humble. My first car, a Saab 900 Turbo, seemed like a very cool vehicle at first. Not long after I got it, I heard a strange noise and suddenly could not drive any faster than 30 mph—not a good situation on a Southern California freeway. The ultimate humility was donating my turbocharged sports car for a fundraising car smash to help out the football team.

I entered my senior year as the starting quarterback with lots of friends and a lot of superficial reasons to be prideful. As a reminder that humility is part of the path to success, God "blessed" me with a "sweet ride"—an old twelve-passenger van we affectionately called Wheezy. It started slowly in the morning and could be heard for blocks.

"Get your ego out of the equation."—MICHELE TURNEY

One night I invented a brilliant idea in my seventeen-year-old mind. My brother, a friend, and I decided to toilet paper another friend's house. Only high schoolers would consider a loud one-ton van a candidate for a stealth operation in a quiet neighborhood. Somehow we pulled it off without getting caught.

Full of confidence and feeling invincible, I decided it would be awesome to go off-roading in my one-ton van at midnight. I aggressively ventured out on this dirt road, which quickly turned into soft dirt that gave way to a muddy soup. I managed to bury the van axle deep in muck.

We tried to dig out, but the hole just kept filling in behind our efforts. We were hopelessly stuck. In my efforts to free the vehicle, I stepped shin deep in mud, filling my right shoe. The police showed up and saw a pathetic sight. My sweatshirt hood was pulled over my head. I had a shoe on my left foot and a flip-flop on my right. The lead officer asked, "What were you doing out here in the field, son?"

"We decided to go four-wheeling," I said, hoping it made sense to the officer.

"In a van?" he replied with astonishment.

The other officer immediately started looking for drugs and alcohol because there was no way that a sober person would do something so brilliant. Well, I proved them wrong.

About then my dad showed up and asked, "What were you doing driving in the field?"

"We thought we could go four-wheeling," I said, hoping it would sound better this time.

"In a van?"

When the tow truck arrived, the driver asked, "So, what were you doing in the field at night?"

"We were four-wheeling."

"In a van?"

Of course, my brother was all too eager to share the results of my brilliant idea, so the next day at church one person after another walked up and asked, "In a van?" I got out with a great story but with very little pride.

Serving Others Leads to Opportunities

At times you will benefit from the success of others' hard work if you have placed yourself humbly under the tutelage of a leader. When you make it your goal to help your boss, your mentor, your coworkers, friends, and even your parents succeed, you raise your value in their lives. When they look good because of your efforts, they are naturally motivated to help you when the time is right.

Jesus introduced this concept in Matthew 11:29 when he instructed his followers, "Take my yoke upon you and learn from me, for I am gentle and humble in heart, and you will find rest for your souls." Jesus borrowed a picture from farmers who would place a yoke on the shoulders of a team of oxen and attach the yoke to a plow or cart. When a new ox was being trained, the farmer would pair it with a stronger, more experienced animal. If the young ox worked with the older ox, the day went smoothly. As long as the younger beast was helping the older one succeed, he was also being prepared to be the lead ox in the future. Serving the older ensured his future success.

> "I believe we are most likely to succeed when ambition is focused on noble and worthy outcomes rather than on goals set out of selfishness."—JOHN WOODEN

God favors the humble. "For those who exalt themselves will be humbled, and those who humble themselves will be exalted" (Matthew 23:12). Are you catching this? You can ride *God's* coattails. Want to be in film? God is a better connection than Steven Spielberg. Want to be in politics? God is a better "in" than the president of the United States. Want to be a writer? God is a better agent than anyone on the best-sellers' list. Want to perform on Broadway or in Hollywood? God is a stronger introduction than anyone holding a Tony, Emmy, Grammy, or Golden Globe. Want to work as an architect? God is bigger than Frank Lloyd Wright. Want to be a top-notch engineer? God is even better than a degree from MIT, Caltech, or Colorado School of Mines.

If you are good with God, you will be good to go and good to grow. He's got connections, resources, methods, and plans that are higher and better than those of any human.

> "The more you lose yourself in something bigger than yourself, the more energy you will have."—**NORMAN VINCENT PEALE**

Go to www.Love-Wise.com/gradplus to read about a leader who moved from servant to superstar leader because he was willing to believe God.

Serving Others Fights Against Selfishness

As you journey through your life, you're going to hear the word *narcissism* quite a bit. It's a popular word that is increasingly being used to describe your generation. For example, social researcher George Barna says in his book *Futurecast*, "The concept of the common good—sacrificing a personal benefit or opportunity to advance the good of the community—is a casualty of war in a society that has become increasingly narcissistic." He also notes that psychiatrists are "reporting that about one out of ten twentysomethings show evidence of narcissistic personality disorder—several times the rate found among other generations."[3]

So what is narcissism? The term comes from Greek mythology where the story is told of Narcissus, a handsome male youth who refused the love of a nymph named Echo. As a punishment, the gods condemned him to fall in love with his own image, and he eventually became enamored with his own reflection in a clear pool. His love for himself dominated his life, and he eventually died alone.

Narcissistic people are in love with themselves and believe life does—or ought to—revolve around them. Did you hear about the narcissistic man who was trying to be more other-focused? He said to his friend, "Well, enough about me, let's talk about you. How do you feel about me?"

Confident or Cocky?

We are big fans of self-confidence because we believe each person has been made in the image of God. However, you live in a world that wants to take you past self-confidence into a life that is all about you.

In contrast, the Bible calls us to an influential life of serving others. As you serve others, they will look forward to having you around and will seek you out for advice. Even greater than all that, God will reward you for the service you perform on behalf of others.

> You, my brothers and sisters, were called to be free. But do not use your freedom to indulge the flesh; rather, serve one another humbly in love (Galatians 5:13).

Do nothing out of selfish ambition or vain conceit. Rather, in humility value others above yourselves, not looking to your own interests but each of you to the interests of the others (Philippians 2:3-4).

Serve wholeheartedly, as if you were serving the Lord, not people, because you know that the Lord will reward each one for whatever good they do (Ephesians 6:7-8).

How can a person tell if he or she is humble? What is your inner cue that pride or selfishness might be developing in your heart? Picture a person you think is proud, arrogant, cocky, narcissistic, egotistical, and stuck on self. How do you feel when you're around them? What do you wish they would say or do differently?

Serving Others Makes You More Believable

You became imitators of us and of the Lord... your faith in God has become known everywhere. Therefore we do not need to say anything about it, for they...tell how you turned to God from idols to serve the living and true God (1 Thessalonians 1:4-10).

Those who serve prove by their actions and attitudes that they are the real deal.

This was the dynamic secret of Mother Teresa, held up as a hero of virtue and respected by the most influential leaders in politics and business. People took notice of her because notoriety was the last thing she was looking for. She committed her life to serve the poor and disadvantaged in India. She was valiant in courageously speaking for those who cannot speak for themselves. She once was asked at a White House dinner, "Why has a woman not been elected President in this land of freedom?" Bravely, she replied, "You probably aborted her."

As a reward for her humble diligence, God chose to exalt her. Her funeral was televised worldwide since millions had been inspired by her selfless devotion to a labor of love. Her description of her life was, "I am a little pencil in the hand of a writing God who is sending a love letter to the world." No one ever questioned her integrity because her service proved that her heart was true.

> "We can do no great things. We can do only small things with great love."—**MOTHER TERESA**

One of our all-time favorite prayers is by Saint Francis of Assisi:

Lord, make me an instrument of your peace;
where there is hatred, let me sow love;
where there is injury, pardon;
where there is doubt, faith;
where there is despair, hope;
where there is darkness, light;
and where there is sadness, joy.

You Live

STRETCH THOSE HUMILITY MUSCLES

Try these exercises for practicing humility in your life:

- Go one day without pointing out to others your contributions or accomplishments.

- All week compliment and encourage anyone who makes you look good or helps you.

- When given a compliment, practice silently thanking God for enabling you to succeed.

- Ask God to show you your potential by choosing to see yourself as he sees you. In your journal, begin to record any verses that help you see yourself the way God sees you.[4]

 Go to www.Love-Wise.com/gradplus to take a quiz to see if you have any traits of a narcissist—then trade it in for being a servant leader and find real success.

@Colin Powell
"A dream doesn't become reality through magic;
it takes sweat, determination and hard work."

@Old adage
"Each day you must choose: the pain of discipline or
the pain of regret."

@Mary Kay Ash
"Ideas are a dime a dozen. People that implement
them are priceless."

@Vince Lombardi
"The dictionary is the only place that success comes
before work. Hard work is the price we must pay
for success. I think you can accomplish anything if
you're willing to pay the price."

Chapter 10

Decide to Finish What You Start

Y ou are embarking on a great journey. No matter your path—success does not happen just because you showed up. Your place of productivity and influence must be secured. It is not automatically handed out simply because of your talent or degree. It takes perseverance, dedication, and a stubborn intention to finish what you start.

> "Today I will do what others won't, so tomorrow
> I can accomplish what others can't."—JERRY RICE

The most profound statement Jesus made on the cross was, "It is finished." The road to the cross was a grueling road, but it was the one that mattered to him.

He was determined to walk in all the victories and all the difficult turns in order to get to the end. Halfway wasn't good enough. Two-thirds of the way wasn't good enough. He had to get to the finish line.

> "Finish well."
> —EVERY PARENT OF A HIGH SCHOOL
> OR COLLEGE SENIOR

Stick to It

As a gymnast in high school, I (Pam) learned that when you dismount any apparatus, you want to plant your feet as though they are stuck with glue to the mat. It is common for a gymnastics coach to call out, "Stick it." Dismounts are not easy. They take full concentration, hours of training, repeated practice, and sheer will to hold everything in place. Life is often like this. Sometimes we just need to stick to it until we outlast every obstacle to our success.

When our son Zachery was ten years old, we signed him up for gymnastics with two of his friends. For the first few weeks, it went well. Then his two friends quit, so he wanted to quit too. But we have a rule in our family that we finish what we start, so we told Zach that he had to go for the rest of the session. He refused, so I carried my son, who was as big as I was, into the gym and said, "You can sit here the whole time if you want, but you will stay in this gym until class is over. You *will* finish."

Years later, when he won a competitive cheerleader scholarship that helped pay for his college, he pulled me aside and said, "Thanks for making me finish, Mom."

"Nothing will work unless you do."—MAYA ANGELOU

You will be tempted to bail, skip a class, sleep in, or "forget" to do homework. You might not feel like going to work or showing up for class. Successful people don't make decisions based on how they feel. Instead, they turn their desires into commitments.

What makes you want to quit? Ask your friends and family, "Have you ever felt like quitting something? Did you? If you stuck it out, what helped you hang in there?"

Finish What You Start—Caleb

My parents were always there to encourage me to finish what I started. "Farrels aren't quitters" is a saying I heard a lot growing up. Without this encouragement, I would not have become the person I am today.

Being extremely shy by nature, I loathed the idea of being the leader of a Fellowship of Christian Athletes (FCA) club at my school. I knew it would be way out of my comfort zone. I have never liked presenting in front of people even though I know it's good for my personal development.

Once I concluded that God was calling me to form a club on campus, I was stuck. If I started this club, I would need to see it through.

I also learned that you can turn a thought into a conviction by repeating it over and over. I had heard that so many times it was lodged in my soul. So I knew I could decide to put my heart and soul into leading this club. I have to admit God made me stronger through this club, and I developed skills I'm sure I would not have learned any other way. So one lesson, one Bible discussion, one speech at a time, I moved my life and the club forward.

> "Small steps taken consistently add up in big ways over time."—DANNA DEMTRE

I went from being a little kid who could not say two words as simple as, "Thank you," in front of a church to a young man who got an A in his college public-speaking class. Don't let these opportunities pass you by because they are hard or uncomfortable. God can shape you in ways you did not think were possible.

> "The most important thing in life is not to triumph but to compete"—PIERRE COUBERTIN

Listen to Your Passion—Brock

"For we are God's handiwork, created in Christ Jesus to do good works, which God prepared in advance for us to do" (Ephesians 2:10).

As a senior in high school, I had plans. I experienced just enough success as a quarterback that I believed I had a shot at a college scholarship. With full-blown determination, I worked hard to improve so I could perform at the highest level possible. The hard work paid off, and I had a successful senior season, leading all of San Diego County in passing yards and efficiency. I even received a visit from a coach at the University of Colorado. But he thought I wasn't tall enough to be a legitimate Division I recruit. He even told my head coach, "You have a good little quarterback there." Signing day came and went, and nobody offered me a scholarship.

That was the first time in my life I experienced the shattering of a dream. The thing I wanted the most was not going to happen, and I sat on the edge of my parents' bed crying. But even though I was discouraged, I wasn't ready to give up the hope of playing college ball.

"There are many ways to the top
of the mountain."—PAM FARREL

Earlier in my senior season, my high-school coach had taken me to a Saddleback College game, and I was impressed with Saddleback's offensive system and had heard good things about their head coach. I thought I might still have a shot at playing at a Division I school if I first went through the community college system.

> "Don't let what you cannot do interfere
> with what you can do."—JOHN WOODEN

At the end of a meeting with the Saddleback head coach, he saw the competitive fire in my eyes and said, "Look, he wants to start competing right now." His statement sealed my decision; I was going to play for the Gauchos of Saddleback College. It turned out to be one of the best decisions I ever made. After two seasons, nineteen wins, the school record for passing touchdowns, and an award for Mission Conference player of the year, I still look back on my time there as the most fun I had playing football.

Those two years also became the springboard to my opportunity to compete at the Division I level. After my sophomore season, I was offered and accepted a scholarship to play quarterback at Liberty University in Lynchburg, Virginia. Although some of my time at Liberty was disappointing from a football perspective, so many other positive things happened in my life during that time that I have grown to be thankful despite the disappointment. I received a quality education, grew closer to God, connected with some impressive coaches, and met my wife.

Now that I have graduated from college, I am forever thankful for the people I met on the less-than-perfect journey. I can see now that this was God's best plan for me.

> "We can do anything if we stick to
> it long enough."—HELEN KELLER

Turn Your Passion into a Career

After graduation, I was contemplating what to do with my life and what direction I wanted to go. I called my dad to talk about my realistic options. He said, "God gives us dreams and a vision for our lives, and sometimes he ends one dream to call us to a new and greater dream, and now you need to find out what that new dream is." This conversation was a breakthrough moment for me. I realized what he was saying was true and it would be in my best interests to pay attention.

I knew the NFL was not an option, but I thought I might have a shot at making an Arena Football team. I participated in a tryout, and although the tryout went well, I chose not to pursue that opportunity.

But sometimes our short-term goals are a reflection of our long-term passions. While I was waiting for the tryout, I decided to start coaching at Liberty Christian Academy (LCA) in Lynchburg. Coaching awakened something in my heart. I loved helping young men get better. I loved being around other coaches who were setting game strategy and planning how to build character in the young men on the team. A newfound sense of fulfillment welled up inside me as I watched these young competitors put into action the skills I had helped them develop. Somewhere along the route the thought occurred to me, *I could do this for the rest of my life. My playing days may be over, but my football days don't ever have to be over.* I just had to be humble enough to accept that this was what God created me for.

How about you? What are you passionate about today? Do you have a short-term passion that has the potential to be the long-term dream that will guide your career decisions? Ask your friends and family:

- "Do you see any small thing in my life that God might want to make a big thing?"

- "Do you have any less-than-perfect experiences that God used to guide you into something you feel successful at today?"

WORK IT OUT

Consider these verses as you ponder how to hang in for the long haul and press toward your desired goal (emphasis has been added):

Let us throw off everything that hinders and the sin that so easily entangles. And let us run with perseverance the race marked out for us (Hebrews 12:1).

Make every effort to add to your faith goodness; and to goodness, knowledge; and to knowledge, self-control; and to self-control, perseverance; and to perseverance, godliness; and to godliness, mutual affection; and to mutual affection, love (2 Peter 1:5-7).

Continue to work out your salvation with fear and trembling, for it is God who works in you to will and to act in order to fulfill his good purpose (Philippians 2:12-13).

You may be on earth at this time in history to create something new, provide compassion for a group of people, train up future leaders, manufacture products that benefit all of us, or support the infrastructure of your community. Your combination of skills, however, is in seed form. They need to be grown, cultivated, and matured in order to have their full impact. That is where perseverance comes in.

Small Beginnings...Big Adventures

I (Pam) got my first writing byline in my junior high school paper. I published my first book in college.

I (Bill) gave my first inspirational message in college and my first sermon at age twenty-six. This past year we published book number thirty-eight, and we were away from home for speaking 220 days.

It doesn't happen overnight. It happens one small goal upon one small goal. Elisabeth Elliot, whose husband was killed in the Ecuadorian jungles trying to reach a primitive people with God's love, was asked how she built a ministry, raised a daughter, and wrote books to become a beloved leader to women worldwide. Her simple advice was, "Do the next thing."

One thing does lead to another.

> "Wisdom is knowing what to do next.
> Skill is knowing how to do it. Virtue is
> doing it."—THOMAS JEFFERSON

What you are doing today might seem like a small beginning, but we are convinced that you are reading this book because you are destined for big things. Soon you will pass through the curtain and take center stage for the role of a lifetime: your calling.

Your unique contribution will become clearer with each passing year if you are looking for it. As your insight into yourself grows, decide to finish what you start so the rest of us can benefit from who you are.

We say "Thanks" ahead of time for becoming all God desires you to be.

"The future belongs to those who believe in the beauty of their dreams."—**ELEANOR ROOSEVELT**

You Live

What is the first small step you want to take as a result of reading this book? Meet with your parents, mentors, and friends, and tell them your plans. There is power in speaking your dreams. The synergy of you, God, and those you love working together will create a life you can look forward to living.

 Go to www.Love-wise.com/gradplus to get your graduation gift from us. Congrats!

Notes

Chapter 1—Decide to Go Big

1. http://zenhabits.net/how-to-be-childlike/.
2. www.forbes.com/2009/02/26/starting-second-career-leadership -careers_dream_jobs.html.
3. http://answers.yahoo.com/question/index?qid=20071211102950AAt SK0V.

Chapter 2—Decide to Use Social Media

1. http://devotionaldiva.com/ministry/.
2. "Top 10 YouTube videos of all time," August 2011, www.readwriteweb .com/archives/top_10_youtube_videos_of_all_time.php.
3. Erin Bury, quoted in "99 Favorite Social Media Quotes and Tips," www .mirnabard.com/2010/04/99-favorite-social-media-quotes-and-tips/.
4. "Facebook Has Big Lead in Avg. Monthly Minutes," www.market ingcharts.com/direct/facebook-has-big-lead-in-avg-monthly-minutes -16699//.
5. Mary Bart, "Do College Students Spend Too Much Time on Facebook, YouTube and Other Social Networking Sites?," *Faculty Focus*, December 30, 2009, www.facultyfocus.com/articles/trends-in-higher-education/ do-college-students-spend-too-much-time-on-facebook-youtube-and -other-social-networking-sites/.
6. www.facebook.com/group.php?gid=115889895093052#!/group .php?gid=115889895093052&v=wall.

7. "Many Teens Spend 30 Hours a Week on 'Screen Time' During High School," *Science Daily*, March 14, 2008, www.sciencedaily.com/releases /2008/03/080312172614.htm.

8. Nicholas Carlson, "How Many Users Does Twitter *Really* Have?" *Business Insider*, March 31, 2011, www.businessinsider.com/chart-of-the -day-how-many-users-does-twitter-really-have-2011-3.

9. Alana Semuels, "Television Viewing at All-Time High," *Los Angeles Times*, February 24, 2009, http://articles.latimes.com/2009/feb/24/ business/fi-tvwatching24

10. "Technolog," MSNBC.com, October 14, 2010, http://technolog.msnbc .msn.com/_news/2010/10/14/5290191-average-american-teen-sends -and-receives-3339-texts-a-month.

11. "Interesting Statistics about Video Games," *DYI Father*, January 29, 2008, http://diyfather.com/content/Interesting_Statistics_About_Video _Games.

12. Derek James, "Kids Addicted to Facebook?" WCCB-TV (Charlotte, NC), March 16, 2010, www.foxcharlotte.com/news/top-stories/87985307 .html.

13. Megan Farokhmanesh, "Facebook Can Lead to Narcissism, Depression in Kids," *Newsy*, August 8, 2011, www.newsy.com/videos/study-face book-can-lead-to-narcissism-depression-in-kids.

14. Tyler Woods, "Women Checking Facebook Before Going to Bathroom," *EmaxHealth*, July 12, 2010, www.emaxhealth.com/1357/women-check ing-facebook-going-bathroom.

15. Jonathan Leake and Georgia Warren, "Facebook Fans Do Worse in Exams," *Sunday Times*, April 12, 2009, www.timesonline.co.uk/tol /news/uk/education/article6078321.ece.

Chapter 3—Decide to Follow Your Heart

1. http://watermarkblogs.org/stories/04/god-is-able/.

2. http://quickfacts.census.gov/qfd/states/00000.html.

3. www.logos.com/22.

Chapter 4—Decide to Be Skilled

1. "Fresh from College, More Grads Moving Back Home," *Huffington Post*, www.huffingtonpost.com/2010/06/21/moving-home-college_n _619181.html.

2. Laura Petrecca, "Toughest Test Comes After Graduation: Getting a Job," *USA Today*, May 21, 2010, www.usatoday.com/money/economy /employment/2010-05-19-jobs19_CV_N.htm.

3. Liz Pulliam Weston, "How to Blitz Your College Debts," *MSN Money*, http://articles.moneycentral.msn.com/CollegeAndFamily/Money InYour20s/HowToBlitzYourCollegeDebts.aspx; Mark Whitehouse, "Number of the Week: Class of 2011, Most Indebted Ever," *Wall Street Journal*, May 7, 2011, http://blogs.wsj.com/economics/2011/05/07/number-of-the-week-class-of-2011-most-indebted-ever/?KEYWORDS=college+graduates.

4. Lev Grossman, "Grow Up? Not So Fast," *Time*, January 16, 2005, www.time.com/time/magazine/article/0,9171,1018089-4,00.html.

5. Shaheen Samavati, "Recent College Graduates Finding Entry-level Jobs Hard to Get and Hard to Keep," *Plain Dealer*, May 31, 2009, updated January 14, 2010, www.cleveland.com/help-wanted/index.ssf/2009/05/recent_college_graduates_findi.html.

6. For a more complete discussion of decision-making, see Bill and Pam Farrel, *The 10 Best Decisions a Single Can Make* (Eugene, OR: Harvest House Publishers, 2011), 9-30.

Chapter 5—Decide to Be Real

1. We are grateful to Bill Bright, founder of Campus Crusade for Christ, for explaining the process of spiritually breathing in a simple, user-friendly way.

2. *LOL with God* (Colorado Springs, CO: Focus on the Family/Tyndale House Publishers, 2010), 28.

3. Inventory at this website is from Gary L. McIntosh and Samuel D. Rima, *Overcoming the Dark Side of Leadership* (Grand Rapids, MI: Baker Books, 1997, 2007).

Chapter 6—Decide to Build a Network

1. Diagrams of spider web construction come from Ed Nieuwenhuys, "The Construction of a Wheel Web," http://ednieuw.home.xs4all.nl/Spiders/Info/Construction_of_a_web.html.

2. Susan M. Heathfield, "Listen with Your Eyes: Tips for Understanding Nonverbal Communication," About.com, http://humanresources.about.com/od/interpersonalcommunicatio1/a/nonverbal_com.htm.

3. www.universalstudioshollywood.com/entertainment_jobs/about_us.html.

Chapter 7—Decide to Invest in Relationships

1. Joe S. McIlhaney and Freda McKissic Bush, *Hooked* (Chicago: Moody Publishers, 2008), 31-32.

2. Ibid., 33,35,43.